An A-Z of Rock and Roll

Graham Wood

Studio Vista London

Acknowledgments

The author gratefully acknowledges the assistance given by the following individuals and companies: Paul Alford; Carlin Music Corporation; Columbia Film Corporation; Harry Dodds of the Gene Vincent Fan Club; Duane Eddy; Rob Finnes; Roger Ford and Hank Taylor of *Rock 'n Roll Collector* magazine; Brian Gear; Charlie Gillett; Dave Gregory of the Conway Twitty Appreciation Society; Bob Howlett of the Larry Williams Appreciation Society; Paul Jamieson of the Buddy Knox Appreciation Society; 'Wild Little Willie' Jeffrey; Malcolm Jones; Gina Marks; MGM Films; Bill Millar; Pete Morgan of the Eddie Cochran Society; 'Waxie Maxie' Needham; David Nelhams of the Rick Nelson Fan Club; Adrian Owlett; Mick Perry; Denis Preston of the Fats Domino Club; *Record Mirror*; Steve Richards; *Soul* magazine; Eddie Tre-Vett; Twentieth Century Fox Films; United Artists Film Corporation; Paul Vernon of the *Sun Legend*; Alan Warner of Liberty Records; Colin Wood.

The quotation on page 7 from *Yakety Yak* by Leiber and Stoller is reproduced by permission of the Carlin Music Corporation.

Published in Great Britain by
Studio Vista Limited
Blue Star House, Highgate Hill, London N19
Set in Plantin 10 on 11 point
Printed in Great Britain by
Robert MacLehose and Co. Ltd
The University Press, Glasgow

SBN paperback 289 70005 1
     hardback 289 70006 X

JIMMY ("JUST A DREAM") CLANTON
SANDY ("MUSIC, MUSIC, MUSIC") STEWART
CHUCK "MABALIENE" BERRY
The Late RITCHIE ("DONNA") VALENS
JACKIE ("LONELY TEARDROPS") WILSON
LIKE I MEAN—
It Swings!
SEE! 10 GREAT ROCK 'N ROLL STARS!
HEAR! 17 GREAT NEW ROCK 'N ROLL HITS!
GO, Johnny GO!
STARRING ALAN FREED The King of ROCK 'n' ROLL!
EDDIE ("COME ON EVERYBODY") COCHRAN
HARVEY of the MOONGLOWS
JO ANN WAIT A MINUTE CAMPBELL
THE SPEEDO CADILLACS
THE "LOVERS NEVER SAY GOODBYE" FLAMINGOES
starring ALAN FREED · JIMMY CLANTON · SANDY STEWART · CHUCK BERRY
SPECIAL GUEST ARTISTS
The Late Ritchie VALENS · Jackie WILSON · Eddie COCHRAN · HARVEY of the MOONGLOWS · The CADILLACS · The FLAMINGOES · JoAnn CAMPBELL

Foreword

Rock and roll will always be
It'll go down in historee.

Certainly. But it is a sobering thought that today's generation of pop lovers is mostly ignorant of the roots of the music they dig. There has been very little documentation of the pre-Beatles musical era. Without rock and roll there would have been no musical revolution in the last decade. Until Elvis Presley and Bill Haley got into the charts, pop was dominated by the sound of the Flabby Fifties. If you ever think the top ten are bad today take a look at the songs that topped the charts before the rock era began. It may be hard to believe but teenagers once hummed such unforgettable melodies as *If I Were A Blackbird*, *In A Shady Nook* and *Hopscotch Polka*.

Rock and roll emerged in the US from an unholy union between white country music and black rhythm'n blues. The result was energy, pace, mood, excitement and style. For total recall Proust needed those curious little biscuits. Me? I prefer to sit through the opening minutes of *Blackboard Jungle*. A blank screen and then Blam! 'One o'clock, two o'clock, three o'clock Rock. . .' Bill Haley whetted the musical appetite of my teenage generation. Distinctive youth culture was still a frail plant in those dim, distant days of the mid-fifties. Just as I was getting ready to jive in the aisles, national service summoned me. That is why rock first came to me filtered through the Tannoy system of a bleak RAF basic training camp in the middle of Staffordshire. The fiercest debates in the billets were over the relative qualities of Tommy Steele's and Guy Mitchell's rival versions of *Singing The Blues*. Suez and Hungary interrupted us for a short period but by the time Soviet tanks had smashed through Budapest we were back to ruminating on the comparative virtues of Elvis's *Hound Dog* and the haunting *Heartbreak Hotel*.

The music for which so many of my contemporaries still have an enormous affection depended for its impact on a quivering energy, a mannerist style of performance and an intimate relationship between singer and audience that today's pop heroes would scorn. The famous pelvis was only one small part of my rock and roll mosaic. There was Eddie Cochran in his gold-lamé suit, Gene Vincent's black leather gear, Chuck Berry with his duck-walk, Jerry Lee Lewis and his piano pyrotechnics. It is easy to mock the illiteracy of rock and roll lyrics. The winds of poetic change had not yet been blown by the Beatles and Dylan. There were no introverted prophets to inscribe nightmarish images on our skulls like Dylan's 'motor-cycle black madonna two-wheeled gypsy queen'.

What we wanted (and got) was music with an irresistible beat. The protest songs of rock and roll were not political but generational.

Take out the papers and the trash
Or you don't get no spending cash
If you don't scrub that kitchen floor
You ain't gonna rock and roll no more
Yakety yak
Don't talk back.

Rock and roll songs preceded the era of youthful revolutionary consciousness.

They were stark songs about cars, work, nagging parents and girls. The outside world was always portrayed as conspiring to prevent rock and rollers from having fun. Indeed fun was a crucial element in the music of the late fifties — fun and those astonishing girls described in a raunchy poetry of Southern gentility. To recall the litany of these girls is enough to make me break out in a sympathetic attack of acne. There was *Long Tall Sally*, *Good Golly Miss Molly*, *Groovy Little Suzie* and *Lawdy Miss Clawdy*.

The rockers themselves developed a style as distinctive as the music they followed. The country's high streets were peppered with drape jackets, winkle-picker shoes, drain-pipe trousers and slim-jim ties. The girls swirled round the dance floors with their pony-tails and crinoline petticoats. In America it was the period of low-slung garrison belts, staying cool and making out in drive-ins. It was a time of innocence when pot was something you put the baby on and fuzz was something you rubbed off fruit. If you really want to know about the fifties just play Gene Vincent's classic *Be-Bop-A-Lula* and listen to his breathy little gasps in the second verse just before the line 'She's the one that loves me so'.

About every six months on the hour the pop pundits tell us that a rock and roll revival is about to happen. But it can never be manufactured as a commodity to sell to today's pop-lovers. They should listen to the original records and remember what preceded and what followed the period covered by Graham Wood in this book. Without Chuck Berry,

Little Richard and scores of lesser known singers there would have been no Beatles, no Rolling Stones and no pop explosion. It is only appropriate that the early groups who first helped to forge the generation gap should be given their historical due.

To understand why the seventies are being described as 'the new fifties' and why there is a reaction against the false complexity of so many progressive groups, you have to return to the original rock and roll. Ask John Lennon about his favourite records and he will tell you about esoteric rock and roll groups like Rosie and the Originals. Sophisticated modern groups swear by their mellotrons and their moog synthesizers in the pursuit of new musical and lyrical boundaries. But as one rock musician told me: most of the modern groups are merely moving to the right and left of the three basic chords of rock and roll.

Nostalgia can, of course, be confused with parody. (It would be revealing to re-run some of the original rock TV shows like Six-Five Special and 'Oh Boy'.) Frank Zappa's Mothers of Invention made a rock and roll record in 1969 under the name of Reuben and the Jets. They called it an album of 'greasy love songs' and 'cretin simplicity'. The album credits one musician with 'lewd pulsating rhythm' and another with 'redundant piano triplets'. You think that's funny, Zappa, but you can't camp my nostalgia out of existence. It's my memories and affection against yours.

Those of us who came to pop via rock will continue to shake, rattle and no doubt roll. We will book into Heartbreak Hotel. We will rave on.

RICHARD GILBERT

Paramount Theatre, New York, Easter 1957

IN PERSON ALAN FREED ™ ROCK AND ROLL STARS
ATTERS · FRANKIE LYMON AND TEENAGERS · RUTH BROWN
KNOX · JIMMY BOWEN · CLEFTONES · NAPPY BROWN · CADILLACS
CHARLES · MAUREEN CANNON · DUPONTS · ROBIN ROBINSON
DON'T KNOCK THE ROCK ™ ·· BILL HALEY AND COMETS
DALE · ALAN FREED TREMIERS · LITTLE RICHARD · DAVE APPELL
IN PERSON A
™ GREAT ST
ROCK "N" R
"DON'T KNO
PARA

An A–Z of Rock and Roll

In 1955 with the arrival on the scene of Bill Haley and his Comets, rock and roll came into its own as a popular music force. Soon practically any band that was playing with a beat was labelled rock and roll, in some cases quite unjustifiably. The sweet sounds of the forties were forgotten as artists fought to get on this new gravy train. Many of the early pioneers of the music became lost in the welter of publicity accorded to the young idols such as Presley, Vincent, Fabian and Avalon, and consequently were never given credit for their early work.

Such artists as Amos Milburn, Matt Lucas, 'King' Curtis Ousley, Charlie Feathers and Roy Brown were rarely mentioned and thus their valuable contributions to the scene were overlooked.

This book deals mainly with artists who contributed to rock and roll between the years 1955 and 1961, but the early pioneers should not be forgotten, for it was primarily owing to their efforts that rock and roll emerged at all.

Paul Anka

Born in Ottawa, Canada, on 30 July 1941, Paul made his first few dollars as a singer at the age of twelve, when along with two friends he performed at local functions during the evenings. The trio achieved a big reputation and were asked to play in theatres and clubs all over Canada.

After a while the trio disbanded and Paul, determined to make it as a professional entertainer, persuaded his parents to send him to Hollywood where he had an uncle with connections in the entertainment world. Eventually he signed to a small Los Angeles label who released

Blau Wildebeeste Fontaine, which went on to sell around three thousand copies.

He finally took a tape of *Diana* and three of his other compositions to Don Costa, then a. and r. head of ABC Paramount Records. Costa was impressed not only with the songs, but with the singer also, and immediately signed Anka to a lucrative contract.

Diana became his first hit, selling over a million and topping the US charts for one week and the UK charts for nine, a record at the time. He followed this with his own composition *You Are My Destiny*,

Paul Anka, 1957

again winning a gold disc. Other recordings to earn gold discs were *Lonely Boy*, *Put Your Head On My Shoulder*, *Puppy Love* and *My Home Town*.

In 1961 Paul starred in his first major film *The Longest Day*, along with a host of international stars. He had also composed the film theme tune.

Paul Anka was the youngest performer ever to star at New York's famous Copacabana Club.

Little Anthony and the Imperials

Formed early in 1958 and consisted of Anthony Gourdine (lead tenor), born 8 January 1941, Clarence Collins (baritone), born 17 March 1941, Ernest Wright (second tenor), born 24 August 1941 and Sam Strain (first tenor), born 9 December 1941. All the members of this quartet were born and brought up in New York.

Whe he graduated from school Anthony joined a group known as the Duponts and recorded the following titles with them: *Must Be Falling In Love*, *You* and *When You Wish Upon A Star*. In 1957 Anthony joined the Chesters, which also included at the time Clarence Collins and Ernest Wright. Anthony recorded *Fire Burns No More* as his only single with the Chesters.

Eventually they were heard by Richard Barrett who changed the name to the Imperials, adding Sam Strain to make up the quartet. They were signed to End Records who released *Shimmy Shimmy Ko Ko Bop* as their debut release. In 1958 *Tears On My Pillow* became their biggest seller and secured the team's only gold disc. Other releases followed, including *Prayer And A Jukebox*, *The Diary*, *Limbo*. They successfully toured

the States and in the early sixties were still a force to be reckoned with in the recording world.

Frankie Avalon

Born Francis Avallone in Philadelphia on 18 September 1940. Frankie learned to play the trumpet while still in the junior grade at school and by the age of twelve was proficient enough to join a band appearing in a summer season in Atlantic City. His performances were seen by talent scouts and he was asked

Frankie Avalon, 1958

to appear on TV shows hosted by Jackie Gleason, Paul Whiteman and Ray Anthony as well as on various radio shows.

After achieving a certain degree of fame as a teenage trumpet prodigy he took up singing also, and was duly spotted by music publishers Bob Marcucci and Peter De Angelis, who signed him to a management and recording contract on their Chancellor label.

His first recording for Chancellor, *Dede Dinah* was a nation-wide hit and sold a million. This led to the usual round of guest spots on the top TV shows and also to Frankie's debut in films, performing *Teacher's Pet* in *Disc Jockey Jamboree*.

Although *Gingerbread* did quite well for him, Frankie had to wait over a year for his next million seller, *Venus*, which was a big seller in England and topped the US charts for five weeks. He followed this with two other million sellers in *Just Ask Your Heart* and *Why* (which was also a big British hit for Anthony Newley).

The following year saw Frankie branching out as as an entertainer, appearing in several top nightclubs as well as making a film appearance in *Guns Of The Timberland*.

Lavern Baker, 1957

Lavern Baker

Born in Chicago on 11 November 1929. Lavern, like many youngsters in her area, joined the local Baptist church choir and by the time she was twelve she had already decided she would try to make a living as a singer when she was older.

At seventeen she signed a contract to appear at Chicago's Club Delisa, for George and Mabel Woods, who billed her as 'Little Miss Sharecropper'.

She was so popular she was asked to stay for six months and during that period she was seen performing by the famed Fletcher Henderson, who was so impressed with her ability that he wrote a song specially for her, *When I'm In A Crying Mood*.

Her next engagement was at the Flame Bar, Detroit, where the manager, Al Green, signed her to a management contract. Green negotiated a tour for her as vocalist with the Todd Rhodes band, during which she was seen by representatives of King Records who signed her to a recording contract. On her first session for King she cut *Trying*, *Pig Latin Blues* and *Must I Cry Again*.

At this point, just as she was beginning to make a name for herself nationally in the US, Lavern made a European tour. She liked Italy enough to stay there for six months, and during her visit she was unofficially 'adopted' by a titled Italian family, which was how she acquired her nickname of 'Countess'.

On her return to the US she signed to Atlantic Records, her King contract having finished. At her first session for Atlantic she cut *Tweedle Dee*, which when released sold thousands on its way

Poster from Rockland Palace, New York, typical package show, about 1959

up the charts. Her follow-up disc was *That's All I Need*, which again made the best sellers.

In 1957 she appeared in two major rock and roll films, *Mr Rock And Roll* and *Rock, Rock, Rock*.

Soon after the success of *Tweedle Dee* Lavern complained to Detroit Congressman Charles Diggs, that her arrangement, which had cost her several hundred dollars, was being copied note for note, and she had lost over $1500 in royalties. Upon investigation Diggs found that singers had no recourse if their material was copied. This led to a study by Congress of the laws that protected singers' copyrights.

Lavern was also a help to another young singer later to achieve fame, Johnny Ray. He was appearing in Detroit, at the Flame Bar where Lavern had been discovered, and asked her advice on how to sing the blues. Lavern generously agreed to help and showed how to get the best out of a song. Johnny soon went on to great things and he attributed much of his success to Lavern's help.

Among other songs recorded by Lavern was *Play It Fair*, which might have been aimed at the people who were pirating her arrangements. Her biggest hit came in 1959 when the fabulous *I Cried A Tear* topped the charts, selling a million and earning her a first gold disc.

Hank Ballard and the Midnighters

Hank Ballard joined the Midnighters (then known as the Royals) in the latter part of 1952.

They were recording for Federal Records and in November 1952 recorded their first side with Hank, *The Shrine Of St Cecilia*, which, backed by Bill Doggett's band, became a minor hit. Their first big hit came in 1954 when they recorded *Work With Me Annie*, the band being Robert Darby (tenor), Sonny Thompson (piano), Arthur Porter (guitar), Alonzo Tucker (bass) and Robert Boswell (drums). This combination plus the group notched up their first million seller. This was followed by *Sexy Ways* and *Annie Had A Baby*, both again million sellers. In October 1954 in one week they had their three big sellers standing at numbers two, six and eight in the US charts, a feat to date not repeated.

In September 1954 they first recorded with their new guitarist, Calvin Green. He was to prove a big asset to the team, his fine guitar patterns complementing their vocal work. This can be noted on *Ring A Ling A Ling* and *I'll Pray For You*. He recorded, on 11 November 1958, a song called *The Twist*, which under Chubby Checker's name became a hit three years later. Other interesting sides are *Sugaree* and *She's Got A Whole Lotta Soul*.

Hank Ballard's work had quite an influence on many of the fifties artists but unfortunately where they advanced musically Ballard did not, as listening to his pre-'62 recordings will prove. Hank and the Midnighters were nevertheless among the finest of the early rock outfits.

Chuck Berry

Charles (Chuck) Edward Berry was born in St Louis on 18 October 1931. He began learning the guitar while he was in High School and by 1952 had formed his first combo.

Chuck Berry on stage, Manchester 1958

At twenty-three he signed with Chess Records of Chicago and in May of 1955 cut his first titles for them, *Maybelline/Wee Wee Hours*, the personnel on this disc (besides Chuck) being Johnny Johnson (piano), Willy Dixon (bass), Jasper Thomas (drums) and Leonard Chess (maraccas). Co-writer of this disc was Alan Freed. This combination proved to be a commercial success and soon Chuck found himself with a gold record to prove it.

His follow-up disc, *Thirty Days/Together*, also with the same personnel, did not have anything like the success of *Maybelline* but simply served to keep

Chuck's name in front of the record-buying public. In 1956 he had his second million seller with *Roll Over Beethoven*, which led to film appearances the following year in *Rock, Rock, Rock* and *Mr Rock And Roll*.

The famous Berry 'duck-walk' was also started in 1956 when he appeared, with his combo, on Alan Freed's show at the Paramount Theatre in New York.

In 1957 Chuck achieved further million sellers in *Schoolday* and the frantic *Rock And Roll Music*, backed by his combo of Johnny Johnson, Willy Dixon, Fred Beelow (drums) with Ellis 'Lafayette' Leake replacing Johnson on piano for *Rock And Roll Music* as he did also for *Sweet Little Sixteen* and *Johnny B. Goode*. Berry was going from strength to strength and even made an appearance at the famous Newport Jazz Festival where he was filmed in *Jazz On A Summer's Day* singing *Sweet Little Sixteen*.

In 1959 Chuck appeared in his fourth film *Go Johnny Go*, this time not only singing but also playing a minor acting role, which revealed another talent as a comedian. By this time he was one of the top rock artists in the US.

Chuck Berry was and still is one of the most copied of the rock and roll idols and certainly was one of the more dynamic performers in the fifties and early sixties. His outstanding guitar work and flair for producing a commercial tune and interesting lyrics also contributed to his success.

Chuck Berry, 1965

Bill Black Combo

Bill Black was born in Memphis on 17 September 1926. He joined Sun Records staff band, playing the double bass, and

Bill Black Combo in *Teenage Millionaire*, 1961

Action shot, Bill Black Combo, club
date in USA, 1962

started on the path to success when he accompanied a young singer, Elvis Presley, on his Sun debut. Together with guitarist Scotty Moore, Bill played on no less than twenty-one of Presley's golden discs besides appearing with him in the films *Loving You* and *Jailhouse Rock*.

In 1959 Bill got his break as a performer in his own right. He was signed to a long-term contract by Joe Cuoghi of Hi Records, together with his newly-formed combo of Carl McVoy (piano), Reg Young (guitar), Jerry Arnold (drums) and Martin Wills (sax).

The first release was *Smokie* (Parts 1 and 2) which went on to sell a million. Successive hits followed with *White Silver Sands*, *Josephine*, *Don't Be Cruel* and *Cherry Pink*. Most of these latter singles featured organ in addition to the previously mentioned line-up.

For three years running he won the 'Most Played Combo' award in *Billboard*, the US trade magazine.

Still at the top of his career, Bill Black died of a brain tumour on 21 October 1965.

The Bluecaps

The Bluecaps were Gene Vincent's backing group in his famous Capitol period of 1956–59 and were the first all-guitar/drums group in the world; also, in 1957, the first all-electric band.

The original (1956) group was formed from the houseband of Radio WCMS, Norfolk, Virginia, where Vincent regularly broadcasted between 1955 and 1956. Line-up consisted of Cliff Gallup (lead guitar), Willie Williams (rhythm guitar), Jack Neal (string bass), and Dickie Harrell (drums).

When Gene Vincent arrived in Nashville for his first Capitol session, producer Ken Nelson had already booked a session band. Nelson listened to Gene's own band, agreed they were capable and dismissed the sessioneers. This band appears on the first four Gene Vincent singles, *Be-Bop-A-Lula*, *Race With The Devil*, *Blue-jean Bop* and *Jumps, Giggles And Shouts* and his first album, *Blue-jean Bop*.

With the success of *Be-Bop-A-Lula* the Bluecaps, who were all country boys, found themselves whisked suddenly into the hurly burly of show business with their home life disrupted by the constant travelling. The strain began to tell on them and the first member to leave was Willie Williams, who was replaced by Paul Peek, a singer and instrumentalist from Atlanta, Georgia. The amended line-up appears on Vincent's second album, *Gene Vincent And The Bluecaps*, with Cliff Gallup still playing lead. However, Gallup also left in October 1956 and the band appeared in the film *The Girl Can't Help It* with stand-in Russell Wilford, who also appears on the cover of the second album. Wilford did not, though, record with the Bluecaps.

In January 1957, Vincent went into hospital in Portsmouth, Virginia for some long-delayed treatment on his leg. He was not discharged until April. He was still popular, despite his three-month absence from the scene, but badly needed another hit record to boost his career. Capitol fixed a session with Gene using a makeshift band comprising Dickie Harrell, Bobby Jones (bass), Buck Owens (lead) with Paul Peek and Tommy Facenda as backing vocalists and 'clapperboys', as Gene called them. The titles they cut were

Lotta Lovin' and *Wear My Ring* which became, in October 1957, a double-sided hit in the US. About this time a permanent Gene Vincent Stage Show was formed with Dickie Harrell, Bobby Jones, Paul Peek and Tommy Facenda, Johnny Meeks (lead guitar) and Max Lipscomb (rhythm guitar). This group appeared with Gene on the Ed Sullivan Show, performing *Dance To The Bop*.

In 1959 Gene and the Bluecaps appeared in their second film, *Hot Rod Gang*. At this time Max Lipscomb was replaced by Grady Owens (co-writer of *Lovely Loretta*) and Dickie Harrell by an unknown drummer. Cliff Simmons had been added on piano, and his exciting keyboard work is in evidence on the *Hot Rod Gang* EP issued by Capitol to tie in with the film release.

Late in 1958 Plas Johnson was brought in for the group's last few sessions together and his excellent sax accompaniment was used in *Say Mama* and *Mabelline*, plus a few others. Bobby Jones was also replaced for these sessions. At the end of 1958, after two years of accompanying Gene Vincent, the Bluecaps split up, each going his own way. So ended one of the most interesting musical partnerships of the period.

Gene Vincent and the Bluecaps, Nashville 1956
left to right Cliff Gallup, Gene Vincent, Willie Williams, Dickie Harrell, Jack Neal

Eddie Bond

Born Edward James Bond in Memphis, Tennessee in 1935.

Eddie began his recording career on the long-since defunct EKKO label of Hollywood, who were also responsible for recording several early sides by the Cochran Brothers (Hank and Eddie). He signed with EKKO in late 1955, and had the following records released on the label: *Double Duty Lovin'/Talkin' Off The Wall*, *Love Makes A Fool (Every Day)/Your Eyes*. Neither of these meant much commercially and the recording contract was cancelled.

In March 1956, with the emergence of rock and roll as a musical force to be reckoned with, Eddie signed for Mercury Records and together with his group, the Stompers, cut *Rockin' Daddy* and the Ray Charles classic *I Got A Woman*. Both of these sides were well received, but like many other rockabilly tunes of the period did not sell well enough to register on a national scale. His next release, three months later, *Slip, Slip, Slippin' In/Flip Flop Mama* sold well enough for Mercury to recognize that this talented artist would break through eventually. Then in September 1956 came another classic from Eddie, *Boppin' Bonnie/Baby, Baby, Baby*, the topside being written by two of the biggest names in rockabilly music, Jody Chastain and Jerry Huffman. At this time Eddie began to take a deeper interest in country music and his subsequent releases for Mercury were more in the country than the rockabilly field.

As well as performing their own stage act, Eddie and the Stompers were also responsible for backing Sun recording artist Billy Riley. They all wore green suits while backing Billy on stage which probably accounts for the 'Little Green Men' who are credited as Billy's backing group on his Sun releases.

In 1958 Eddie left Mercury and the following February had *Can't Win For Losing/When the Jukebox Plays* released on the small Stomper Time label. His next release for this label was *Bop Bop Da Caa Caa/You'll Never Be A Stranger (To Me)*, both very much in the country and western field.

By 1960 Eddie was an established country performer recording for many small labels in this field. He now works for Radio KWAM, Memphis, where he has several times been voted number one c. and w. DJ.

It is interesting to note that while he was performing on rock and roll shows he appeared at a show in Ellis Auditorium, Memphis, with Jerry Lee Lewis, Carl Perkins and Warren Smith, and was as well received as any of these greats.

Eddie Bond, 1957

Gary U.S. Bonds

Born Gary Anderson in Jacksonville, Florida, on 6 June 1939. He began singing when he joined the local church choir at nine.

At the age of thirteen Gary was gaining experience by singing in different churches and with different choirs. In 1952 he formed his own group, the Turks, becoming a solo artist when it disbanded. For a long period following this Gary sang in local night clubs in the Norfolk, Virginia, area, finally meeting Frank J. Guida, head of the Norfolk recording studio, who felt Gary had great promise as a singer. A recording contract was negotiated with the LeGrand label and *New Orleans* was set as the first title.

Gary decided to change his surname to something he felt people would remember and seeing an advertisement for Government bonds decided that U.S. Bonds would be a good choice.

New Orleans was released and immediately leapt into the US and UK charts, although not making the top spots. His follow-up *Not Me* did not make much impact. His third release *Quarter To Three* was a smash hit all over the world and stayed for two weeks in the number one spot in the US.

Pat Boone

Born Charles Eugene Boone in Jacksonville, Florida, on 1 June 1934. Shortly before he was two the family moved to Nashville where he eventually attended High School along with his brother Nick, later to become popular as Nick Todd of 'Tiger' fame.

He made his first public appearance at the age of ten in Nashville's Bell Meade Theatre. By seventeen he was hosting his own radio programme on station WSIX Nashville. At eighteen he was the

Pat Boone, 1959

winner of the East Nashville Talent
Contest, the prize being an audition for
the Ted Mack Amateur Hour, and he
subsequently won first place on the Ted
Mack Show three times in succession.

On returning home he married Shirley
Foley, daughter of country star Red
Foley. In February 1954 he enrolled in
the North Texas State Teachers College
in Denton. He studied by day and
performed in the local clubs in the
evenings.

In the summer of that year he was
signed by Randy Wood of DOT Records,
after winning on the Arthur Godfrey TV
Show, making his recording debut with

Pat Boone, 1957

Two Hearts, Two Kisses. His follow-up *Ain't That A Shame*, sold over a million, earning Pat nation-wide acclaim. At the beginning of 1956 Pat was a permanent member of the Arthur Godfrey Show and was also studying at Columbia University, New York, meanwhile turning down the many film offers he was receiving.

This changed the following year when he signed a contract to appear in *Bernadine* following that with *April Love*. These roles soon won him acclaim as the number three box office attraction.

On 3 June 1958 Pat graduated from Columbia University with a BA in Speech and English. In November of that year he appeared in the Royal Command Performance at the London Coliseum. His recording career was extremely successful with million sellers in *I'll Be Home*, *I Almost Lost My Mind*, *Friendly Persuasion*, *Remember You're Mine* in 1956 and *Love Letters In The Sand*, *Don't Forbid Me*, *Why Baby, Why*, *April Love* and *A Wonderful Time Up There* in the following years. Further film appearances came in *Mardi Gras*, *State Fair* and *The Main Attraction*. His sole million seller of 1961 came with *Moody River*.

Big Bopper

The Big Bopper was born Jape Richardson in Sabine Pass, Texas, on 29 October 1938. He grew up in Beaumont, Texas.

He first went into show business through his job as a disc jockey on KTRM Radio in Beaumont where he was swiftly voted number one DJ on the station. It was at this time that he adopted the name by which he was later to become famous. He was eventually made programme director and began songwriting seriously. He sent some demonstration discs of his songs to Pappy Daily, famous record producer from Houston. Daily signed Jape to a recording and songwriting contract with Mercury Records who duly released *Beggar To A King/Crazy Blues* and *Monkey Song/Teenage Moon*, all under his real name. Neither of these singles made any impact and Jape decided to try again with fresh titles.

However, his career was interrupted by his call to join the US Army. On his discharge he rejoined his old station and continued his songwriting, eventually coming up with *Big Bopper's Wedding/Chantilly Lace*. It was the B side, *Chantilly Lace*, which attracted all the attention, entering the US charts in August 1959. It went on to reach the number six spot in the US while climbing to number twelve in the UK, finally earning a gold disc.

He was killed in a plane crash on 3 February 1959 while touring with Buddy Holly, Ritchie Valens and Dion and the Belmonts.

Big Bopper, 1957

Gene Vincent and Joe Brown in ATV's
Boy Meets Girls, 1960

Joe Brown

Joseph Roger Brown was born in Swarby, Lincolnshire on 30 May 1941. Shortly afterwards his family moved to London.

During his early teens Joe developed a keen interest in music and with the coming of the skiffle music trend joined a local-based amateur group known as the Spacemen.

His break came when he was booked by impresario Larry Parnes as guitarist accompanying young hopefuls auditioning for a resident's spot on producer Jack Good's TV series, Boy Meets Girl. Good was immediately impressed, not with the young singers, but with Joe's personality and outstanding instrumental ability. The result was a residency for the series and a management contract with Parnes, who was already grooming several other youngsters for stardom. A recording contract with Decca was negotiated and *People Gotta Talk/ Comes the Day* became the first release. The follow-up *Darktown Strutters' Ball* achieved the lower reaches of the British charts. His TV appearances with such top acts as Eddie Cochran, Gene Vincent, Johnny Cash from the US and Britain's Cliff Richard, Marty Wilde and Billy Fury demonstrated his ability to shine on equal terms with any of the local or imported stars. His backing group the Bruvvers, consisting of Brian Dunn (rhythm), Bobby Graham (drums) and Peter Oakman (bass) also became respected as a top outfit.

Joe eventually left Decca to join Pye. After achieving minor success with *What*

Joe Brown and the Bruvvers (Peter
Oakman, Brian Dunn), 1960

left to right Gene Vincent, Joe Brown,
Billy Fury, Eddie Cochran, 1960

A Crazy World he finally topped the British hit parade in 1962 with *Picture Of You*.

Johnny Burnette

Born John Joseph Burnette in Memphis, Tennessee, on 25 March 1938. His early days were spent in poverty as his parents struggled to find money to feed and clothe Johnny and his brother Dorsey, five years older.

During his first year at High School, Johnny was involved in an accident, receiving serious injuries. He was in hospital for three months. On his return to school Johnny, who was by this time a very useful guitarist, formed a band playing at school and outside functions. However the band folded when the time came for Johnny to leave school.

Johnny and Dorsey became interested in boxing and made quite a name for themselves on the pro circuits with Johnny becoming known as an outstanding welterweight prospect while Dorsey became a Southern champion at his weight. But the brothers soon tired of this method of earning a living and decided to leave the game. Dorsey made his way back to Memphis while Johnny travelled from place to place as a casual labourer.

Finally he returned to Memphis where he joined Dorsey at the local Crown Electric Company working alongside another youngster who was to achieve fame, Elvis Presley. The two brothers also became friendly with another employee, Paul Burlisson, who had a reputation as a fine guitarist. Again Johnny tired of being in one place too long and took to the road. He spent many months away doing a variety of jobs, including working as a deck hand on the Mississippi river boats, but returned to Memphis with the intention of forming a group.

He persuaded Dorsey to leave Crown Electric and after locating Paul Burlisson talked him into joining them.

The three practised hard for some weeks, and then approached local recording chief Sam Phillips for an audition. They duly auditioned but were turned down as Sam thought Johnny sounded too like one of his other discoveries, their friend Elvis Presley. This setback did not, however, deter them. The three bought a car and headed for New York.

Many hours were spent trudging around from agents to recording managers before they finally landed themselves a spot on the famous Original Amateurs Hour show. They appeared and this time duly won, earning themselves a spot on a three-week package tour as a prize. On their return to New York they signed with Harry Jerome, a well known orchestra leader and one of the few people they had heard of back in the South, who immediately fixed them a contract with Coral Records.

Their first session for Coral on 7 May 1956 produced *Tear It Up/You're Undecided*, backed by Dick Jacobs and his orchestra, which was released as their first single. This first release was not the smash hit they had hoped for, even with the help of a personal appearance on the Steve Allen Show.

They signed for the mighty GAC booking company and were one of the acts featured in a three-month touring show. At the completion of this tour they returned to the studios and cut, among other tracks, *The Train Kept A' Rollin'* and *Honey Hush*. *The Train Kept A' Rollin'* when issued became a big

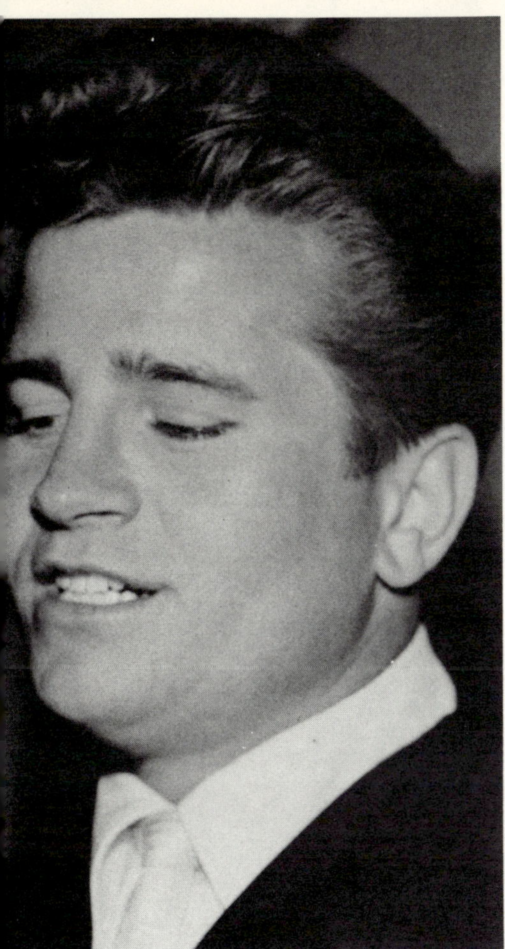

Johnny Burnette, 1960

seller in both the Baltimore and Boston areas, though unfortunately not breaking on a national basis.

They were next signed to appear in the rock film *Rock, Rock, Rock,* which was yet another attempt by the big movie studios to cash in on the rock and roll boom. They were asked to feature their current release, the exciting *Lonesome Train.* Not having much success with the trio single-wise, Coral decided to issue an LP, *Johnny Burnette Rock And Roll Trio* (later issued in Britain on the Vogue-Coral 10 in. series), which sold moderately well. In 1957 the trio broke up with Dorsey leaving to go solo. Johnny and Paul, however, stayed with Coral until the following year when Paul decided to bow out of show business. After looking around Johnny finally signed for the small Freedom label on a short-term contract, releasing without success the singles *Kiss Me, I'm Restless, Gumbo/Me And The Bear, I'll Never Love Again* and *Sweet Baby Doll.* During this period Freedom were bought by the giant Liberty label who acquired Johnny's contract. Johnny was at this time writing songs in conjunction with Dorsey and they wrote the B side of Ricky Nelson's third million seller, *Waitin' In School* Ricky's fourth million seller the following year, *Believe What You Say,* was written entirely by Johnny. He cut two nondescript singles for Liberty, *Settin' The Woods On Fire* and *Patrick Henry* before coming up with his million-selling *Dreamin'/Cincinatti Fireball* in 1960. His follow-up to this *You're Sixteen/I Beg Your Pardon* also sold very well on both sides of the Atlantic.

Johnny and Dorsey Burnette are also thought to have cut records for other labels under the name of the Texans, including *Warm Love* and *My Honey* on Imperial.

Johnny died on 14 August 1964 after a fishing accident.

Freddy Cannon

Born Freddy Picariello in Lynn, Massachusetts, on 4 December 1940. His father was a band leader and during his teens, Freddy formed a small band who used to perform in and around Boston, and on occasion was vocalist with his father's band.

In April 1959 Frank Slay Jr and Bob Crewe, composers and producers of many hit records, in Boston on a business trip, were approached by Boston disc jockey Jack McDermott and asked to listen to McDermott's young discovery, Freddy Picariello.

The two were so impressed they arranged for Freddy immediately to make an audition tape, which they took back with them to New York to listen to. The result was that Freddy was summoned to New York and signed a recording contract with Swan Records. He was given a new surname more in keeping with the image the publicity men wanted to foster.

The first record for Freddy Cannon was *Tallahassee Lassie*, an up-tempo beat number written by Slay, Crewe and Freddy Cannon. The B side was the beat ballad *You Know*. On its release in May 1959 *Tallahassee Lassie* swiftly attracted attention from disc jockeys all over the US and in no time it was in the charts.

He made his TV debut on the Dick Clark Show, following it with the usual round of appearances. His follow-up,

Freddie Cannon with Sounds Incorporated, 1961

Okefenokee, was again a big seller, and the third disc, *Way Down Yonder In New Orleans*, sold a million, earning Freddy his second gold disc.

He visited Britain in 1960, appearing in a couple of TV shows and winning new fans in the process.

Johnny Cash

Johnny Cash was born in Rison, Arkansas, on 26 February 1932. Shortly after his birth his family moved to Dyess, Arkansas, where he spent most of his youth.

After leaving high school he joined the air force and was eventually stationed in Germany. During this period Johnny found time to write many songs, performing them occasionally to his service friends. After completing his service he went to a radio school in Memphis and also auditioned for Sam Phillips. Phillips, seeing in his songs commercial possibilities, signed Cash and his accompanying musicians (Marshall Grant and Luther Perkins, known as the Tennessee Two) on a long-term contract. Johnny's first Sun release was in 1955 with *Hey Porter/Cry, Cry, Cry*. The disc sold very well, entering the top ten of the country charts, as did the following release, *Folsom Prison Blues/So Doggone Lonesome*.

He began appearing regularly on the Louisiana Hayride show in Shreveport, Louisiana, before joining the famous Grand Ol' Opry in Nashville the following year. Around this time he also earned his first gold record for a million sales of *I Walk The Line/Get Rhythm*. Before this he had written a rock song, *Rock 'n Roll Ruby* which was successfully recorded by another Sun artist, Warren Smith. Johnny's first pop-slanted hit, *Ballad Of A Teenage Queen*, came in 1958; this was backed by another Cash composition, *Big River*, both sides serving to show his prowess as a commercial songwriter.

Johnny's final disc for Sun was *Sugar Time/My Treasure*. In 1960 he signed with CBS, one of the largest US labels, recording for them *All Over Again/What*

Johnny Cash, 1958

Do I Care as his first release. By this time Johnny was one of the most popular US country artists, pulling in great crowds on his personal appearances. He also was the first country artist to gain the distinction that all of his first ten releases made the top ten of the country charts. Today Johnny Cash is still at the top of his chosen profession, a position he looks like occupying for years to come.

The Champs

The Champs consisted of Chuck Rio (tenor sax), Dave Burgess (lead guitar), Gene Alden (drums), Van Norman (bass) and Dale Norris (guitar and piano).

A number of members were already recording artists in their own right before joining the Champs; Chuck Rio had already recorded with his group the Originals, Dave Burgess cut a few discs as a solo artist and both Dean Beard and Jimmy Seals, who later joined the group, had recorded before. However, when they all joined together they formed one of the finest instrumental outfits in the US and were soon in great demand for personal appearances.

They signed for the Challenge label (later to record Gene Vincent) and hit number one with their first release, *Tequila*, which stayed at the top of the US charts for five weeks, eventually earning their gold disc. They followed this with *El Rancho Rock* which did not do as well for them. Changes followed in the line-up, Jimmy Seals taking over tenor sax spot, Dean Beard on piano and Dash Croft on drums. They remained a prolific recording outfit, having minor hits such as *Twenty Thousand Leagues*, until the early sixties when they eventually disbanded.

Ray Charles

Ray Charles Robinson was born in Albany, Georgia, on 23 September 1932. He was blinded by illness at six and orphaned by the time he was fifteen. By seventeen he had formed his own trio, with himself on piano, which toured the clubs.

Eventually he settled for a short time in Seattle and landed his own TV show there. He signed for Atlantic Records, his first disc to make any impact being *I've Got A Woman*, which was released

Ray Charles, 1963

in January 1955. Late in 1955 he also came out with a tune which was to remain among his favourites, *Greenbacks*.

His big hit came in 1959 with the classic *What'd I Say* which earned his first gold disc. Turning out one good record after another, he earned the nickname of 'the Genius'.

In 1960 he left Atlantic to sign with ABC Paramount and immediately came up with his second million seller *Georgia On My Mind*. The following year gold disc number three came with *Hit The Road Jack*, which topped the US charts for two weeks.

Apart from the piano Ray Charles also plays alto sax, clarinet and organ.

Jimmy Clanton

Jimmy Clanton was born at Baton Rouge, Louisiana, on 2 September 1940.

After leaving school he formed his own band, the Rockets, of which his brother Ike was a member. They were spotted by talent scout Cosimo Matassa, who arranged for them to audition for the New Orleans based Ace label. Their initial Ace release, *That's You Baby/I Trusted You*, became a regional best seller. The second release, *Just A Dream*, really brought them to national prominence, selling over a million copies, as did their next offering, *Letter To An Angel*. Other releases such as *Ship On A Stormy Sea*, *My Own True Love* and *Go, Jimmy, Go* all helped to establish Jimmy and the Rockets as teen idols.

In 1959 Jimmy starred in his first film, *Go, Johnny, Go*, following this with an appearance in *Teenage Millionaire* in 1961.

His final appearance on Ace was with *What Am I Gonna Do/Am I*. Shortly after this he faded from the recording scene.

Dee Clark

Dee Clark was born in Blythsville, Arkansas, on 7 November 1938. In 1940 his family moved to Chicago where he attended the Farren Grammar School, and after moving again he eventually graduated from Calhoun Grammar School.

In 1952 Dee joined the Hambone Kids and had *Hambone* issued on the OKEH label. His mother, Delecta, is also featured on this disc. In 1954 he was with the Goldentones on their Jay Dee release *Run Pretty Baby*, followed by spells with the Kool Gents on Vee Jay. *You Know* and *The Convention* were among releases.

Calvin Carter, noted a. and r. man, saw great potential in Dee as a solo artist and helped him to obtain his first solo record, *Kangaroo Hop/Gloria* on Falcon.

Finally he achieved his first hit with *Nobody But You*, followed by *Just Keep It Up* and *Hey Little Girl* on Abner.

The Clovers, 195?

Jimmy Clanton in *Teenage Millionaire*, 1961

In 1961 Dee achieved a long-awaited ambition with *Raindrops* (Vee Jay), which earned his only gold disc.

The Clovers

Organized while all members were students at Washington DC High School. Consisted of John 'Buddy' Bailey (lead tenor), Matthew McQuater (second tenor), Harold 'Hal' Lucas Jr (baritone), Harold Winley (bass) and Bill Harris (guitar).

After a short period they went to Lou

Krefetz, a local record and music merchant, who listened to them and agreed to act on their behalf. Krefetz took them all to New York for an audition he had arranged with Atlantic Records. Atlantic liked what they saw and heard and signed them to a lucrative recording contract. Their first record in July 1951, *Don't You Know I Love You*, became a huge hit and they found themselves rushed into television and personal appearances. In 1952 the team was broken up by lead singer Buddy Bailey's call-up to join the US Army in Korea. During his absence the lead vocals were handled first by Charlie White and then Billy Mitchell. These temporary substitutions enabled the group to carry on with recording and personal appearances, and they had another hit in 1953 with *Yes It's You*. Buddy rejoined the group in the summer of 1954, and with Buddy back as lead voice, they enjoyed yet another big seller with *Blue Velvet*, released in February 1955. In 1958 the Clovers had one of their biggest hits with *Love Potion No. 9* which achieved high placings in the US and UK charts.

Not much has been heard of the Clovers for the last few years, and they are thought to have disbanded.

The Coasters

Formed in October 1955, consisting of two former members of the Robins, Bobby Nunn and Carl Gardner, together with Billy Guy, Leon Hughes and Adolph Jacobs. Billy Guy was originally part of a comic singing duo, Bip and Bop, while Leon Hughes was previously with the Lamplighters. In an interview a few years ago Cornelius Gunter claimed that at one point both Guy and Hughes had also been members of the Robins. Adolph Jacobs was a guitarist from Oakland, California.

After the Coasters' first release for ATCO Leon Hughes and Bobby Nunn left the group and were replaced by Cornelius Gunter, a very experienced singer who had been with several top vocal teams, and Bill 'Dub' Jones. The new team were all featured on the second ATCO release, *Down In Mexico*, which quickly became a hit and certainly made the public aware of the Coasters.

ATCO insisted, for reasons unknown, on releasing publicity material of the Robins and labelling it the 'Coasters' until mid-1958. So while the Coasters on record were Billy Guy, Carl Gardner, Bill Jones and Cornelius Gunter, trade magazines, and the public, were led to believe that the line-up was still that of the Robins (Gardner, Nunn, plus, according to Gunter, Hughes and Guy).

Their next release, *Searchin'/Young Blood*, took off, after a slow start, with most DJs playing the B side, *Young Blood*, eventually selling over two million copies and becoming one of 1957's most successful releases. With this hit record behind them the Coasters, like any act with a big seller, did the usual shows all over America and soon became noted for their excellent live performances.

Their follow-up record was *Yakety Yak*, written by the Leiber-Stoller team, who were turning out many hits of that period. It shot up the charts in both the US and UK, earning the team their second gold disc. The Coasters could do no wrong record-wise and their following three releases all sold around the million, *Charlie Brown*, *Along Came Jones* and *Poison Ivy*, again all Leiber-Stoller compositions.

The Coasters (Robins-Coasters picture), 1958

By late 1959 the tide began to turn and their record sales dwindled, *Run, Red, Run* and *Little Egypt* not having half the success of their earlier releases.

In 1960 Bill 'Dub' Jones left the team and was replaced by Nathaniel Wilson, a former member of the recording group the Shields. Perhaps the most incredible thing is that for all their hits, unlike many one-hit wonder groups, the Coasters did not appear in any of the vast number of rock films of the 1955–60 period.

Eddie Cochran

Eddie Cochran was born in Oklahoma City on 3 October 1938. He was the youngest of five children. Shortly after his birth his family moved to Albert Lea, Minnesota, where they remained until he was eleven.

In 1949 his family moved to California, where he eventually joined a local group and became noted for his excellent guitar work. It was during this period that he met Connie 'Guybo' Smith who later became his bass player. In 1956 together with his cousin Hank he recorded for the California-based Ekko label, releasing three singles, *Tired and Sleepy*, *Mr Fiddle* and *Guilty Conscience*. These singles were released as the Cochran Brothers and are now extremely rare collector's items. His first solo effort came later that year on the Crest label, *Skinny Jim/Half Loved* (later released on Liberty after being polished up). This was followed by three singles for Silver (who operated from the same address as Crest, an instrumental credited to the Kelly Four, *Strollin' Guitar/Guybo*; plus a couple of singles with Jewel Akins (of *Birds and Bees* fame), *Opportunity* and *Doin' the Hully Gully*, under the name of Jewel and Eddie. He finally signed with Liberty and cut *Sittin' In The Balcony* as his initial release. This really set the charts on fire and eventually sold a

Eddie Cochran in *Boy Meets Girls*, 1960

Eddie Cochran on stage, Chevron, Nebraska, 1957

million, earning Eddie star status. As a
result he was chosen to appear in *The
Girl Can't Help It* performing the
exciting *Twenty Flight Rock*. It was on
this set that he first became friendly with
Gene Vincent. He achieved his next gold
disc when *Summertime Blues* became a
smash on both sides of the Atlantic in
1957, following this with yet another
million seller in *C'mon Everybody*. Further film appearances followed in *Untamed Youth* and *Go, Johnny, Go*.

Finally in 1960 he was booked to
appear in England on a tour, headlining
together with his friend Gene Vincent.
He made his final appearance at Bristol

Eddie Cochran in Boy Meets Girls,
1960

Hippodrome on 16 April 1960. The following day the car in which he was travelling to London Airport was involved in a crash. He was killed and Gene and Sharon Sheeley were seriously injured.

Eddie left a selection of memorable performances both on disc and film. He will also be remembered as one of the first performers to play, by means of multi-recording techniques, more than one instrument on his records.

Dave 'Baby' Cortez

Born David Clowney in Detroit, 1939. He attended North Western High School in Detroit where he began to take an

Dave 'Baby' Cortez, 1957

interest in learning to play the piano. His father was an accomplished pianist and encouraged him. He joined a vocal group, the Pearls, who became fairly well known.

He was seen by a talent scout and signed for the New York based label Clock and with his second release on that label, *The Happy Organ/Love Me As I Love You*, he hit the charts both in the US and UK. His subsequent releases (among them *The Whistling Organ*, *Piano Shuffle* and *Deep In The Heart Of Texas*) did not register, except for *Cat Nip* which caused a minor impact.

Sonny Curtis

Born in Meadow, West Texas, on 9 May 1937. Made his first public appearance at a country music concert in Lubbock, Texas. His reputation as a guitarist and vocalist grew with every engagement, and he made his radio debut on KSEL, Lubbock, in 1951. His television debut was made three years later on the local KDUV station.

On graduating from high school Sonny headed for Nashville as a member of Buddy Holly's Three Tunes. His fine guitar work was in evidence on Buddy's early sessions for US Decca where he is heard on the following tracks — *Blue Days*, *Black Nights*, *Love Me*, *That'll Be The Day* and *Rock Around With Ollie Vee* (which he wrote). Sonny decided to stay in Nashville where he became sought after as a session guitarist, also finding time to back Slim Whitman and Buddy Knox on their live appearances in the area. He also signed a recording contract with DOT Records and released the following singles — *Wrong Again/Laughing Stock* and *Pretty Girl/Willie Mae Jones*.

Shortly after Buddy Holly's death in 1959 Sonny was asked by Jerry Allison and Joe B. Maudlin to join them as lead vocalist and guitarist in the Crickets. The group was at this time still based in Lubbock under the management of Norman Petty. His first record as lead singer with the Crickets was *Baby My Heart/More Than I Can Say* on Coral.

For a long period following the release of this record nothing was heard from the Crickets until in May 1960 Sonny, Jerry and Joe arrived unannounced in England as the backing group for the Everly Brothers who were making a nation-wide tour. During the following winter Sonny was drafted into the US Army serving in France. He still, however, found time for songwriting and penned *Walk Right Back* which was a big hit for the Everly Brothers.

Bobby Darin

Born Walden Robert Cassotto in East Harlem, New York, on 14 May 1936. Bobby was a sickly child and did not attend school until he was eight because of bouts of rheumatic fever and other ailments. He eventually won a scholarship to the Bronx High School of Science, and during one summer vacation he met fellow student Donnie Kirschner, who had recently obtained a contract for

songwriting. They teamed up and within a short space of time won a contract writing and singing commercials for a New Jersey radio station.

Eventually Bobby was offered a contract as a singer by Decca Records who released *Rock Island Line* (a cover of the Donegan version). This and later Decca

Bobby Darin, 1958

singles soon faded away and eventually Bobby joined Atco, a subsidiary of Atlantic Records.

He wrote *Splish, Splash*, together with Jean Murray, and in 1958 this became his initial Atco release and his first million seller.

Other hits came with *Queen Of The Hop* (also a gold disc winner), *Mighty Mighty Man, Early In The Morning, Dream Lover* and *Mack The Knife* (the last two both 1959 million sellers). Bobby acquitted himself well on his TV and live appearances with his amazing versatility (playing vibes, guitar and drums besides dancing and singing) which eventually led to film contracts. He appeared in *Pepe, Too Late Blues, Come September, Hell Is For Heroes* and *If A Man Answers*.

By 1961 Bobby was one of the world's highest paid entertainers, touring successfully in both Britain and Australia. He also found time to marry actress Sandra Dee.

The Del–Vikings

In 1955, five young servicemen, Clarence Quick, Corinthian 'Krips' Johnson, Chuck Jackson, Donald Backus and David Lerchey decided to form a group. A year after they had formed they entered the air force's Tops in Blues contest.

They won and while stationed in Pittsburgh signed a contract with the Fee-Bee Company and recorded over a dozen songs for them, including *Come Go With Me, Whispering Bells, Don't Be A Fool*, and *How Can I Find A True Love*. The lead vocal alternated between Krips Johnson, the main lead, Chuck Jackson and white singer Gus Backus. Fee-Be leased *Come Go With Me, Whispering Bells* and *Willett* to DOT Records.

Come Go With Me was a big 1957 hit, selling a million, and overnight the group became stars. The appearances that followed on ABC TV's Circus Time and Rock 'n Roll Revue consolidated their position as a top vocal team.

Willett met with only a little success, with the label crediting the number to Chuck Jackson, not the Del-Vikings.

The group finally left Fee-Bee when their contract expired, though Fee-Bee still released a couple more Del-Vikings' singles (now credited to the Original Del-Vikings). The group next recorded an album for Luniverse Records which was withdrawn after a law-suit concerning a re-recording of *Come Go With Me* that appeared on the album. Chuck Jackson left and gradually new members joined, making the group an almost all-white outfit. They went on to record for Mercury, Alpine, ABC Paramount and Gateway before disbanding.

The Del Vikings, 1957

Bo Diddley

Born Ellas McDaniel in McComb, Mississippi, on 30 December 1928. He was taught the violin by Professor O. W. Frederick, musical director for Ebenezer Baptist Church in Chicago.

Soon after he entered high school he joined a three piece band playing violin. At seventeen he switched to the guitar and made his professional debut in 1951 at the 708 Club in Chicago. In June 1955, while working in Chicago with his combo, he was spotted by Leonard and Phil Chess and was signed to their label, Checker. Shortly after he wrote and recorded *Bo Diddley*, which became his first hit. He became noted for his guitars, which were all shapes and sizes, and his amplification equipment which he designed himself. He made his New York debut with the Dr Jive Rhythm and Blues Review at the famous Apollo Theatre in 1955.

Other notable recordings were *I'm A Man*, *Diddley Daddy*, *Pretty Thing* and *The Clock Strikes Twelve*. Most of his records were his own compositions and were backed by his sister, 'the Duchess' and Jerome Green.

Dion and The Belmonts

Born Dion Di Mucci in the Bronx, New York, 18 July 1940. Like many of his friends he learned to play the guitar, and he made his professional debut at eleven.

When he was seventeen he decided together with his friends Fred Milano, Angelo D'Aleo and Carlo Mastrangelo to form a vocal group which they called the Belmonts. They went for an audition with the New York-based Laurie Records and were immediately offered a contract.

Their first disc for the label did not cause any great reaction from popular music circles but sufficiently encouraged their recording manager to give them *I Wonder Why*, a song in which he had great faith, as their next song. Shortly after its release it began to pick up sales, gathered momentum and eventually ended up in the charts. After this, appearances on all

Dion in *Teenage Millionaire*, 1961

Bo Diddley and 'the Duchess', 1968

the top TV and radio shows followed, helping their next three releases *No One Knows*, *Teenager In Love* and *Where Or When* to appear in the best sellers' lists.

Then in 1960 after three successful years together Dion and the Belmonts decided to part company. Dion realized that the boys were eager to build a stronger identity as a group while he was keen to explore further entertainment avenues. They divided, Dion notching hits on the ABC Paramount label with *Lonely Teenager*, *Runaround Sue*, *The Wanderer*, *Drip Drop* and *Ruby Baby*, while the Belmonts found success with *Tell Me Why*, *Come On Little Angel*, *Don't Get Around Much Anymore* and *I Need Someone*.

Bill Doggett

Bill Doggett, probably the first organist to hit the charts playing rock and roll, comes from Philadelphia. His 1956 combo signed for King Records and he found himself with a million seller in *Honky Tonk* (Parts 1 and 2). He became much in demand after this and notched up a string of successful dates.

Other big sellers were *After Hours* and *Big City Drag*, *Snuff Box* and *Leaps and Bounds* (Parts 1 and 2).

Fats Domino

Born Antoine Domino in New Orleans on 26 February 1928, one of a family of nine. His father was a violinist and an uncle, Harrison Verrett, played with many New Orleans bands including those of Kid Ory and Oscar Celestin. When Fats, as he was nicknamed, was five a brother-in-law left a battered piano to the family and Fats practised for hours attempting to master the rudiments of piano playing. He formed his first band at ten from a group of friends.

At fourteen Fats started work cutting lawns in and around New Orleans. This was hard work for little reward, so he eventually got himself a job in a local factory that made bed springs. He was still practising hard at the piano and even playing some of the local honky tonks during some evenings.

Then Fats' hand became entangled in a machine at the factory and was badly damaged. The doctors advised an amputation, but Fats, determined to keep his hand at all costs, refused and embarked on a long series of exercises in order to recover the strength and feeling, and he finally recovered.

Fats then married his childhood sweetheart, Rosemary, who, realizing how much he wanted to play professionally, urged him to accept dates at the local Hideaway Club. After a while Fats joined the group there, led by bassist Billy Diamond, becoming so popular that people used to come from miles to hear Fats playing. Finally news of his performances reached the ears of Lew Chudd, president of Hollywood's Imperial recording organisation. Chudd travelled to New Orleans to see for himself and was so impressed he offered Fats a long-term contract.

Fats met Dave Bartholomew, a. and r. man with Imperial, and found they had a mutual interest in songwriting. They began turning out some excellent numbers and chose one of them, *The Fat Man*, for Fats' first release. The line-up for this session was probably as follows: Domino (vocal and piano), Dave Bartholomew (trumpet), Joe Harris (alto), Herb Hardesty (tenor), Alvin 'Red'

Fats Domino and band on stage of London's Saville theatre, 1966

Fats Domino, 1958

sales, and really established Fats with the record-buying public.

Fats made his film debut in *Do Re Mi* in 1956, following it with appearances in *Shake, Rattle and Rock*, *Jamboree*, *The Girl Can't Help It* and *The Big Beat*. By 1960 Fats had over seventeen gold discs to his credit making him, along with Elvis Presley, one of the top-selling rock artists in the world.

The Drifters

The Drifters were formed when Clyde McPhatter left Billy Ward's Dominoes in late 1953 with the idea of starting his own vocal group. The original team consisted of: Gerhard Thrasher (tenor), Billy Pinkney (bass), Charlie Hughes (baritone) and, of course, Clyde McPhatter as lead vocalist.

In March 1954 their initial release, *Money Honey*, on Atlantic became a hit. This was quickly followed by *Such A Night* and Clyde's own composition *Honey Love*. After these disc successes they were signed to appear twice a year for ten years at the Apollo in New York. After a year with the group Clyde McPhatter left to join the US Armed Forces. Before leaving, however, he tasted success with his last disc, *Whatcha Gonna Do*.

Tyler (tenor), Clarence Hall (tenor), Ernest McLean (guitar), Frank Fields (bass) and Earl Palmer (drums). The combination was enough to produce Fats' first million seller, the first of many successes to come for this composing team. The follow-up disc *Goin' Home*, did equally well, again reaching a million

The Drifters continued as a trio for the next three years before going their own ways in mid 1958. On sessions they were occasionally augmented by the inclusion of David Baughan. *Drip Drop*, released in 1958, was the group's final recording with the old line-up. The group's manager, George Tredwell, was left to find a group to fulfil the yearly Apollo contracts.

Treadwell signed the New York-based Crowns and renamed them the Drifters, the line-up being Ben E. King (lead), Ellsbury Hobbs (bass), Charlie Thomas (tenor), Doc Green (tenor). Their first disc, *There Goes My Baby*, was the first hit for the re-formed act, quickly followed by *Dance With Me*, *This Magic Moment*, *Lonely Winds* and *Save The Last Dance For Me*, and others. After *Save The Last Dance For Me*, Ben E. King left the group and the lead was

The 1957 Drifters line-up
left to right Bobby Lee Hollis, Gerhard Thrasher, Andrew Thrasher, Billy Pinkney

The 1960/61 Drifters line-up
left to right Gene Pearson, Johnny Terry, Charlie Thomas, Johnny Moore and Billy Davies

handed over to Rudy Lewis. Hobbs left (for the services) at the same time, and Tommy Evans joined for a while in his place. Rudy Lewis is featured on *I Count The Tears*.

Today the Drifters are still functioning, albeit with a totally different line-up from the original, and on their earlier recordings they have left some of the finest examples of fifties' vocal work.

Duane Eddy

Duane Eddy was born on 26 April 1938 in Corning, New York, but was brought up in Phoenix, Arizona. He began learning to play the guitar when he was five, and began to take it seriously when he was fifteen and playing in local groups. He graduated from Coolidge High School in Arizona, at the time not intending to play music professionally.

In 1957 he joined a group run by Al Casey (later to be one of Duane Eddy's own group, the Rebels) and also began studying the guitar under well known jazz guitarist Jim Wybele. He was spotted playing by top independent producers Lee Hazlewood and Lester Sill, and made a couple of demonstration discs for them which they took to Jamie Records of Philadelphia. They immediately signed Duane to a recording contract and within a short time his first single, *Movin' 'n Groovin'*, was issued. The unique sound of his guitar began to cause an impact with local DJs, and *Movin'* became a minor hit. He was at this time touring with the original Rebels who consisted of Steve Douglas (sax), Al Casey (bass) and Mike Beramann (drums). His second offering, *Rebel Rouser*, was an instant hit and eventually went on to sell a million, giving Duane his first gold disc.

He made his TV debut on Dick Clark's Saturday Night Show and was an outstanding success. Changes had by this time taken place in the Rebels with Jim Horn replacing Steve Douglas and Dave Campbell taking over on drums. Further hits followed with *Ramrod, Cannonball, The Lonely One, Peter Gunn, Forty Miles of Bad Road*, etc.

He made his film debut in 1960 in *Because They're Young*, performing the title tune, which also sold a million and was a smash hit on both sides of the Atlantic.

In 1962 his popularity began to wane as he was no longer turning out the exciting sound of the early days. But Duane had by then already earned his place in the record books as the first instrumentalist to sell over three million records in his first year of recording.

The Everly Brothers

The Everly Brothers, Don and Phil, were born on 1 February 1937 and 19 January 1939 respectively, in Brownie, Kentucky.

The Everly Brothers, 1966

Their parents, Ike and Margaret, were well known country singers, and when they were still children they performed and appeared on shows with their parents. Their parents retired when the boys finished at high school and the two of them decided to perform as the Everly Brothers. They were spotted by Columbia Records and signed to a contract. Their first release, in February 1956, was *The Sun Keeps On Shining/ Keep A Lovin' Me*. It did not register and eventually the boys left the label.

Shortly after they signed a management deal with Wesley Rose of the famous Acuff-Rose Publishing Company in Nashville. He signed them to another recording contract with Cadence, who released *Bye Bye Love* which became a million seller. Their second release, *Wake Up Little Susie*, earned their second gold disc and really established the boys as a top act. They were swiftly whisked to New York for appearances at the Paramount Theatre, and on the Perry Como Show and Ed Sullivan Show. The following year (1958) brought their

Duane Eddy, 1957

biggest fifties' seller in *All I Have To Do Is Dream/Claudette*, which topped the charts in the US for four weeks and in Britain for nine. That year also brought gold discs for *Bird Dog* and *Problems*. *Take A Message To Mary* and *Till I Kissed You* added to this list the following year. In 1960 they finally left Cadence for the newly formed Warner label, making their debut with *Cathy's Clown*, which eventually turned out to be their best-selling single. It topped the US charts for five weeks and British top ten for nine weeks. It earned their eighth gold disc and was penned by the boys themselves. A Sonny Curtis composition, *Walk Right Back*, won their ninth gold in 1961.

'The Everly Brothers were the first of the popular vocal duos of the fifties to make a real impact. This was mainly owing to their fine harmony and the commercial songs provided by Felice and Boudleaux Bryant.

Fabian

Born Fabiano Forte in Philadelphia on 6 February 1943.

In September 1957 he was discovered by Bob Marcucci (who together with partner Pete De Angelis owned Chancellor Records and also managed Frankie Avalon) who set about grooming him for stardom. In the ensuing months Fabian spent hours learning to sing, a task which he never really mastered. Eventually after a couple of disc flops, *I'm A Man* hit the charts. His position as a star was consolidated by the next release *Turn Me Loose* which again hit the best sellers. Dick Clark's ABC audience voted Fabian 'Most Promising Male Singer of 1958', and the following year he earned a gold disc for his rendering of

Tiger (also recorded by Pat Boone's brother Nick Todd), following that with a double-side smash with *Come On And Get Me/Got The Feeling*.

He signed a film contract, making his debut in 1959 with *Hound Dog Man* followed by *High Time*, *North To Alaska* in 1960 and *Love In A Goldfish Bowl* in 1961.

By 1962, however, Fabian was already a has-been with the fickle record buyers and left the record business to concentrate on a film career.

Charlie Feathers

Charlie Feathers was born in Hollow Springs, Mississippi on 12 June 1932. At nine he was given his first guitar and spent many hours practising playing and singing country tunes. After leaving school he took a job on a pipeline and in

Fabian, 1958

1953 was taken ill with spinal meningitis, staying in hospital for over a year before he fully recovered.

Eventually Charlie auditioned for Sam Phillips and Sun Records and was immediately accepted. His first release, *I've Been Deceived* and *Peepin' Eyes* was on the Flip subsidiary (a label launched to test local reaction to Sun artists). His only Sun waxing was *Defrost Your Heart/Wedding Gown Of White*. He made his radio debut on WMPS Memphis at this time, promoting his release. Shortly after he left Sun, he released *Tongue Tied Jill* on Meteor Records and made his TV debut on the Wink Martindale Show on Channel 13 in Memphis.

By this time he was very much a local personality, having successfully appeared in a rock show at the local Overton Shell Park together with Elvis Presley, Johnny Cash and Wanda Jackson. After Meteor he moved to King where he released many fine sides including *When You Decide*, one of his personal favourites.

Other releases followed on Kay, *Jungle Fever*, *Why Don't You*, etc., and Walmay (under the name of Charlie Morgan), *Dinky John*.

Charlie Feathers may never have had a major hit disc but certainly was among the more important of the Memphis artists.

The Flamingos

The Chicago-based group the Flamingos consisted of Jacob Carey, Zeke Carey, Paul Wilson, John Carter and Sollie McElroy. They first recorded for the small Chance label, their first disc being *If I Can't Have You*. The following year they moved to Parrott, recording *On A Merry Way* as their first single. Nate Nelson had joined by this time, replacing Sollie McElroy as lead vocalist.

In 1955 they signed with Checker of Chicago, making their debut with *That's My Baby*. By 1956 they had already established themselves and had tasted chart success with *I'll Be Home* (the Pat Boone number). Over the course of the next two years the Flamingos established themselves via their hit records and live performances as one of the leading vocal

The Flamingos, 1969

groups in the US. Foreign audiences first saw them when they appeared in the film *Rock, Rock, Rock* in 1957.

Also in 1957 Zeke Carey and John Carter left the act to pursue solo careers, being replaced by Tommy Hunt (vocals and pianist) and Terry Johnson (vocals and guitar), two very able musicians. They also left Checker and signed a contract with the giant Decca label. Their first release on Decca was *Let's Make Up/The Ladder of Love*, which was issued in the UK on Brunswick. Neither of these songs made much impact, and after nearly two years with Decca releasing such numbers as *Hey Now*, *Jerry Lee*, *Helpless*, *The Rock 'n Roll March*, they decided to leave.

A new contract was singed with End Records, their first release being *Lovers Never Say Goodbye*, which they featured in their second film, *Go, Johnny, Go*

(as yet unreleased in the UK). Zeke Carey had re-joined the group at this time and was featured on this record.

The Fleetwoods

The Fleetwoods consisted of Gretchen Christopher born 29 February 1940, Barbara Ellis born 20 February 1940, both from Olympia, Washington, and Gary Troxel born 28 November 1939, from Centralia, Washington.

They first formed at High School and decided to try as professionals after audiences had remarked on their excellent harmony work. They eventually signed with Dolton Records and achieved two number one records and gold discs with *Come Softly To Me* and *Mister Blue*.

The Fleetwoods, 1958
left to right Barbara Ellis, Gary Troxel, Gretchen Christopher

Frankie Ford

Frankie Ford was born in Fretna, Louisiana, on 4 August 1940. He attended the Southeastern College, Hammond, forming a band with some fellow students.

He eventually joined Huey Smith and the Clowns as one of the leading vocalists and was featured on their many live and filmed appearances.

In 1959 he decided to go solo and joined Ace Records where he sold a million with his first release, *Sea Cruise*.

Connie Francis

Born Concetta Franconera in Newark, New Jersey, on 12 December 1938. She was educated at Newark Arts High School and Belleville High. She learned to play the accordion while she was still at high school and first entered show business at eleven as a singer/accordionist on the Startime show on TV. A year later she entered and won the Arthur Godfrey Talent Scout Show. Eventually Connie was chosen by George Scheck to be featured vocalist on his Startime series. She was signed by MGM Records in 1955 and together with Marvin Rainwater earned her first gold disc for *Majesty of Love*. She continued to record, as a solo artist, turning out well produced records which did not, though, appeal to the popular market, with the exception of *Sailor Boy* which became a minor hit. Finally in 1957 her father suggested she might try recording an 'oldie' with a beat. *Who's Sorry Now* was given the revival treatment and in a short time had brought a second gold record. She began making the rounds of all the popular radio and TV shows, besides becoming in demand for tours both in the US and overseas.

Chart successes also came with other recordings such as *I'm Sorry I Made*

Connie Francis, 1959

You Cry, Stupid Cupid, Carolina Moon, Lipstick On Your Collar, Among My Souvenirs, Robot Man, Mama, Everybody's Somebody's Fool, My Heart Has A Mind Of Its Own, Where The Boys Are.

She made her film debut in 1961 with a part in *Where The Boys Are,* also going on to star in the sequel *Follow The Boys.*

She was unique in that during her first two years as a major artist she consistently gained higher chart placings, on the average of each record release, in Britain than in the US. Not only was she voted top female vocalist in America, but in England too she was voted top female singer in the world, an honour which she won three years running.

Alan Freed

Alan Freed was born on 15 December 1922 in Johnstown, Philadelphia; he displayed an interest in music fairly early on and began learning to play the trombone.

He formed his first band while he was still in high school, naming them the Sultans of Swing, and began playing dates in and around Salem.

After high school he enrolled in Ohio State University taking a course in journalism. Soon, however, he changed to an engineering course and it was while studying this that he first became interested in radio announcing.

In 1941 he was drafted into the forces but after only a few months' service he was taken ill with mastoiditis and was discharged the following year with impaired hearing.

He eventually landed a job with Radio WKST in Newcastle, Philadelphia. However, this particular station catered almost entirely for classical music followers, and although it gave Alan an

excellent grounding in radio station work it was not particularly the kind of music he wanted to play over the air. Eventually he joined Radio WAKR in Akron as a sport announcer. His break came when the DJ for the night show failed to arrive and he was asked to take his place for the show. He was such a success he was hired to host the show regularly. He left over a year later and joined Radio WJW in Cleveland where he met the man who was to help his career rocket to new heights. Leo Mintz, owner of the largest record store in Cleveland noticed that 'race' (or blues) records were beginning to sell in large quantities, particularly the up-tempo items of this music. He advised Freed to include some of these discs in his programmes. They were such a success that Alan renamed the music Rock 'n Roll, calling his show 'Rock 'n Roll Party'.

In March 1952 he staged a 'Moondog Ball' in Cleveland. The venue only had a 12,000 capacity and 30,000 fans turned up. This was probably the first riot caused through a rock show. The show was called off with many disappointed fans turned away. Freed staged many of

   Alan Freed, 1957

these shows while he was in Cleveland, all to sell-out crowds.

In April 1953 he was involved in a serious car accident which kept him sixteen weeks in hospital and then three months at home. He still continued to broadcast, though, from a chair beside his bed.

In 1954 he joined WINS, New York, making his debut on 8 September with the King Of the Moondoggers Show. Soon after he changed the name to that of his old show 'Rock 'n Roll Party'. He also began building talent through the dances and shows he promoted in the area.

In 1955 he made his film debut in *Rock Around The Clock* following this with appearances in *Rock, Rock, Rock, Mr Rock And Roll* and *Go, Johnny, Go*.

He died from uremia on Wednesday 20 January 1965 in Desert Springs Hospital, Palm Springs, California.

Alan Freed will be remembered by many as the champion of rock and roll music. He also was a good songwriter. He composed *Maybelline* for Chuck Berry and also cut several discs with his band for Coral Records, including *Teen Rock* and *Rock 'n Roll Boogie*.

Billy Fury

Born in Liverpool on 17 April 1941 and christened Ronald Wycherley. He grew up in the tough district of Dingle and after leaving school first worked in an engineering works as tea-boy. After this he got a job working on a tug and in his spare time formed a skiffle group with some friends.

His first appearance was at the Essoldo Cinema, Birkenhead, where promoter Larry Parnes was presenting his Rock

Extravaganza show. He approached Parnes to let him do a short spot which Parnes agreed to do. He was such a success that Parnes kept him in the show, after signing him to a management deal and changing his name.

In a few weeks he was signed by Decca to a long-term contract, releasing *Maybe Tomorrow* which made the top twenty within a short time. Also successful were his next few releases, including *Margo, Don't Knock On My Door, Collette* and *My Advice*. Many of them were also his own compositions.

In many towns where he appeared his stage act created uproar for being 'too suggestive', so that late in 1960 he publicly announced he would clean it up.

In 1961 he had his greatest disc success with *Halfway To Paradise* which soared high into the charts, eventually selling over a quarter of a million copies.

He was also twice voted runner-up to Cliff Richard in national polls.

Charlie Gracie

Born Charles Graci in Philadelphia on 12 January 1936. While he was still at junior school his father began teaching him how to play the guitar. When he graduated from South Philadelphia High he was keen to enter the music business and took two recordings he had made in a makeshift studio to the local Cadillac label. Soon *Boogie Boogie Blues/I'm Gonna Sit Right Down And Write Myself A Letter* was released, credited to Charlie Graci (the only time his correct name was used on a record label). The disc flopped and Cadillac did not ask him for any more tracks. His next release turned up on Town and Country Records, *Honey, Honey/Wildwood Boogie*. During a tour promoting this disc Charlie was spotted by scout Bernie Lowe, who had just launched Cameo.

Charlie signed and saw his first release *Butterfly* soar into the best sellers and earn a gold disc, even though both sides were covered by other artists, *Butterfly* by Andy Williams and *Ninety Nine Ways* by Tab Hunter, with versions that were also hits. His follow-up *Fabulous*, although not earning a gold disc as did its predecessor, reached the US top ten and also number four in the UK.

In August 1957 Charlie appeared at the London Palladium, promoting his latest disc *Wanderin' Eyes*, which again sold very well. When he went back to the US he was featured performing *Cool Baby* in the film *Jamboree*.

Eventually Charlie began to do more night club work and slowly drifted from the public gaze.

Charlie Gracie, 1957

THE KINGS OF ROCK
ARE ROLLIN' BACK TO THE SCREEN...
IN THEIR
BIGGEST!
BILL HALEY
AND HIS COMETS
The stars who made headlines in every continent on earth in "Rock Around The Clock"... now bring you the biggest rock 'n' roll ball of all!
co-starring
ALAN DALE
Don't Knock The Rock
Sensational story ...music and romance — with THE BEAT!
ALAN FREED
THE TRENIERS
LITTLE RICHARD
DAVE APPELL
AND HIS APPLEJACKS
Written by ROBERT E. KENT and JAMES B. GORDON · Produced by SAM KATZMAN
Directed by FRED F. SEARS · A CLOVER PRODUCTION · A COLUMBIA PICTURE
with JOVADA and JIMMY BALLARD

Bill Haley

Bill Haley was born in Highland Park, Michigan, in 1927. When he was seven years old the family moved to Booth Corner, Pennsylvania. Bill, not having yet made any friends in the new area, spent most of his time constructing a pasteboard guitar.

Bill's first job came when he was thirteen — entertaining at a local auction for one dollar a night. By the time he was fifteen he was earning his own living from music and at seventeen decided to leave home to try and make his fortune as a musician.

He played in many different bands, working in pubs and little honky tonks in the country, and even joined a medicine show for a while. He ended up with the Down Homers, who were based in Hartford, Connecticut.

Bill then spent six years as musical director of radio station WPWA in Chester, Pennsylvania, and it was during this time that he first began writing songs. In 1953 he started his own band and called them the Comets: Rudy Pompelli (tenor sax), Al Rex (bass), Francis Beecher (lead guitar), Ralph Jones (drums, later replaced by Don Raymond), Johnny Grande (accordion), Billy Williamson (steel guitar). They were signed to Decca Records and in 1954 released *Crazy, Man, Crazy*, which was an instant hit; this was followed up by a tune Bill had written and which was used in the film *Blackboard Jungle* — *Rock Around The Clock*. This was the tune that really put Bill on the map internationally. It sold over a million copies in the US, Canada and Europe and led to Bill and the Comets starring in their first major

Bill Haley and the Comets, 1956
left to right Rudy Pompelli, Ralph Jones, Bill Haley, Al Rex (*front*) Francis Beecher, Billy Williamson

Bill Haley on stage, Albert Hall, London 1968

film, *Rock Around The Clock* (which grossed more at the box office than any musical previously produced by Columbia Pictures).

Their first television show was *So You Want To Hear A Band*, then later appearances followed on the Milton Berle Show and Ed Sullivan's Toast Of The Town series. Success followed success, another film *Don't Knock The Rock* and hit records among them *See You Later Alligator*, *Rip It Up*, plus a world tour. From 1954 until late 1967 their total record sales were estimated at more than ten million. A tour of Britain in 1957 played to packed houses and was a great success. However, since that tour his only hit record in the UK has been a revival of *Rock Around The Clock*.

Dale Hawkins

Dale Hawkins was born in Goldmine, Louisiana, on 22 August 1938 and christened Delmar Allen Hawkins. As a youngster he picked cotton with the black field hands and after work would sit and listen to their songs and stories.

At eighteen he was playing dates around the Shreveport area making his radio debut on the local KWKH station. He cut a rough demo of *See You Soon, Baboon*, which eventually found its way into the hands of Leonard Chess of the Chess/Checker labels.

He was offered a contract with Checker and *See You Soon, Baboon/Four Letter Word* was issued as his first single. This record really started things happening for Dale, and with his next release, *Susie Q/Don't Treat Me This Way*, he hit the best sellers. His follow-up, though, did not mean much (*Baby, Baby*, featuring James Burton on guitar), and

although he turned out some more good singles for Checker the only ones really of note were *La Do Da Da*, *My Babe* and *Yea Yea* (Class Cutter). He was fortunate in having some fine guitarists on his live and recording sessions, such as Fred Carter Jr, who left to join Dale's cousin Ronnie Hawkins' Hawks, Carl Adams, Kenny Paulsen and Roy Buchanan, who was responsible for the exciting sounds on *My Babe*.

Dale eventually left Checker in April 1961 and joined the Tilt label, where he turned out some interesting sides.

Screamin' Jay Hawkins

Born in 1929 in Cleveland, Ohio, and christened Jalacy Hawkins, he spent his first few years in an orphanage, until he was adopted. At six he began learning to play the piano and during his school-days also took up the saxophone, quickly becoming quite proficient.

On leaving school he became a boxer, winning the 1947 Golden Gloves competition before turning professional. After serving in the US forces, he finally retired from the sport in 1953 to concentrate on a musical career.

His first break came in 1954 when he was spotted performing by Fats Domino, who asked him to tour with him and his band. Jay was such a success with his wild act that he decided to go solo. He was signed by Gotham records, and cut for them *Why Do You Waste My Time* and *Coronet Boogie*, besides a few nondescript singles, but he did not stay long with the label.

He was gradually building a following in the US through his appearances on the Alan Freed Rock 'n Roll Extravaganzas, touring with such stars as Carl Perkins,

Screamin' Jay Hawkins, 1968

Chuck Berry, Jerry Lee Lewis and Bo Diddley.

His next recording venture was with Timely Records, where he cut *Baptize Me In Wine* and *I Found My Way To Wine* as his only singles, before joining Apollo (probably a subsidiary of Timely), where his first release was the B sides of both of the preceding titles, *Not Anymore* and *Please Try To Understand*, the follow-up being in both cases *Baptize Me In Wine*.

Next he signed for the giant Mercury label, releasing *She Put The Wamee On Me/This Is All* as the only single. His prolific output of recordings was continued by a release on Grand, *Take Me Back/I Is*, before settling with Okeh where *I Put A Spell On You/Little Demon* became his initial (and most popular) release.

In the early sixties he ceased touring after falling foul of the law and moved to Hawaii where he bought a night club.

Screamin' Jay with his exotic wardrobe was one of the wilder members of the rock fraternity.

Ronnie Hawkins

Ronnie Hawkins, the last of the original rock 'n rollers, was born on 10 January 1935 in Huntsville, Arkansas.

His family moved to Fayettesville where Ronnie attended the local high school, before graduating to the University of Arkansas.

He formed his first group, the Hawks, in 1952 and used to sing at times with a friend of his, Harold Jenkins (later called Conway Twitty).

After his national service he released his first disc on the Quality label, *Bo Diddley/Love Me Like You Can*.

Ronnie Hawkins and the Hawks on stage, Toronto 1968

The following year (1959) he gained an audition with Joe Reisman of Roulette Records in New York. Reisman was sufficiently impressed with the performance to sign Ronnie on the spot and he immediately recorded *Forty Days/ One Of These Days* as his debut single for the label. Ronnie's group on this session consisted of Will 'Pop' Jones (electrified piano), Levon Helm (drums), Jimmy Ray Paulman (guitar) and a session musician on sax. The disc sold very well nationally and eventually reached the number nine position in the best sellers in Canada.

Ronnie was based at this time in Canada and in fact did most of his work there. His follow-up disc, *Mary Lou/ Need Your Lovin'*, did very well there, again reaching ninth in the best selling discs. In January 1960 Ronnie visited Britain and appeared on Jack Good's Boy Meets Girl show as a special guest promoting his *Southern Love* release on US's Columbia label.

Even with the waning of interest in rock around 1961, Ronnie and the Hawks, thanks to their exciting and highly original stage act, still maintained their popularity in Canada.

Buddy Holly

Born 7 September 1936 and christened Charles Hardin Holley. Buddy Holly has, since his tragic death in the early hours of 3 February 1959 in an air crash near Mason City, Iowa, become one of the greatest legends in popular music.

The youngest of four musically inclined children, he became interested in country and western music at an early

Buddy Holly, 1957

Buddy Holly and the Crickets, 1956

Buddy Holly and the Crickets in Jack
Payne's Off The Record BBC TV show,
1957

age, and by his mid teens had teamed up with school friend Bob Montgomery, and was entertaining at local parties and dances near their home town of Lubbock, Texas. They became a popular local attraction and were eventually given a spot on local radio station KDAV which was followed by a regular series (the Buddy and Bob Show) plus a tour of the south-west with Hank Thompson. His big break, however, came when he appeared on a bill with Elvis Presley, who was on one of his first tours at the time, and as a result was offered a contract with US Decca.

In January 1956 Holly made his first discs for Decca in their Nashville studios, using on some tracks his own band the Three Tunes who consisted of Sonny Curtis, Jerry Allison and Don Guess. When these early efforts failed to make any impact he teamed up with his friends Joe Mauldin and Niki Sullivan, and together with Jerry Allison re-recorded one of their joint compositions in March 1957, under the direction of his new producer and future manager Norman Petty, in his Clovis, New Mexico, studio. When the disc was finally released it gave the group (now known as the Crickets) a number one smash hit with their very first release, *That'll Be The Day*. Between September 1957 and February 1959 Buddy Holly signed as a solo artist to Coral and the Crickets (with Holly as lead singer, on US Brunswick) had eleven hit parade entries in England, besides US chart placings, and at one time in 1958 Holly was featured on four different singles in the English top twenty at the same time, a feat only surpassed in the rock field by Bill Haley some time earlier.

Despite his death at the age of twenty-two, Holly's name was not forgotten, for the 'discovery' of unreleased studio recordings and the overdubbing of backings on to private demo tapes led to

Mrs L. Holly (Buddy Holly's mother), 1962, dealing with correspondence from Buddy's fans after his death

Cutting from the *Los Angeles News*, 3
February 1959

a stream of hits all round the world between 1959 and 1964.

Holly's influence has been reckoned by many to have been as great as that of both his idol, Elvis Presley, and his idolizers, the Beatles. The 'British sound' of the early sixties was very largely based on the imitation and adaptation of the Buddy Holly 'Tex-Mex' sound, and many of the pop idols of that era (among them Tommy Roe, Bobby Vee, Adam Faith and Mike Berry) rose to fame on the strength of imitating his style.

Holly was one of the first white rock stars who relied exclusively on his own material for singles, and he wrote more than a third of his recordings. His vocal style was totally unlike anything of his time and he can claim responsibility for popularizing the lead guitar, rhythm guitar, bass, drums line-up that was later to become the standard. He was also probably the first rock singer to regularly double track his voice and guitar and was also the first singer to use strings on a rock record.

Johnny and The Hurricanes

Johnny Paris (leader and saxophone), Paul Tesluk (organ), Dave Yorko (guitar), Lionel 'Butch' Mattice (electric bass) and Bill Savich (drums), formed one of the most prolific hit recording instrumental groups of the fifties, Johnny and the Hurricanes.

Johnny, Paul, Dave and 'Butch' first met in school in Toledo, Ohio, where they all shared a common love of music. They formed a band playing at school and outside functions.

When the boys left school they were signed to a long-term management contract with a large booking agency. A recording contract was negotiated with Warwick Records and their first single, *Crossfire*, was released shortly after. It became a best seller within weeks.

Johnny and the Hurricanes cutting
Reveille Rock, 1959

The song chosen for their next crucial release *Red River Rock*, not only sold a million in the US, but also earned the group a silver disc in Britain.

Autumn 1959 gave them their third hit in a row with the release of *Reveille Rock*. Their first album became a big seller, establishing them as the top instrumental group in the US.

Soon after these hits they signed for Big Top Records, releasing *Down Yonder*. However, although this single was a hit the public did not buy any of their following releases in anything like the quantities needed to make the best-selling charts, and Johnny and the Hurricanes slowly slipped into obscurity.

The Impalas

Dick Wagner, Tony Carlucci, Lenny Renda and Joe Frazier comprise this vocal team who came to public notice in 1958 with their hit recording of *Sorry*. All the members come from Brooklyn, New York. They chose their name after the parents of one of them bought a Chevrolet Impala. They signed with CUB Records in 1958 and with their first recording found themselves with a million seller. Further releases such as *Oh What A Fool*, *Peggy Darling*, and *All Alone When My Heart Does All The Talking* (as Speedo and the Impalas) followed, none, though, achieving a great degree of commercial success.

The Impalas, 1958

Little Willie John

Little Willie John was born in Camden, Arkansas, on 15 November 1938. During his mid teens he sang with the bands of Duke Ellington, Count Basie and Paul Williams.

By seventeen he had signed for King Records, his first disc being *Fever*, which became a gold disc winner. His fifth disc in 1958, *Talk To Me, Talk To Me*, won his second gold and served to establish him among the top dollar earners on the professional music circuits.

Although his subsequent releases failed to make the Hot Hundred, he still turned out some fine sides for King such as *Let's Rock While The Rockin's Good*, *Leave My Kitten Alone* and *Sleep*. Many of the top singers at the time copied Willie's vocal inflections and even his arrangements, but scarcely anyone improved on his performances.

He was imprisoned in 1966 on a manslaughter charge and died, aged thirty, at the Washington State Penitentiary on 26 May 1968.

Buddy Knox

Buddy Wayne Knox was born in Happy, Texas, on 20 July 1933. It was while he was at the West Texas State College (studying Psychology and Business Administration) that his interest in music really developed. He had taught himself to play guitar as a child and now he became friendly with two other students, Jimmy Bowen who played bass and Donnie Lanier who also played guitar. They formed a trio and began to play at dances on and off campus, with considerable success.

When they left college they added to the group Dave Allred, a drummer and DJ on Dumas, Texas, local radio. At Norman Petty's Clovis, New Mexico, studios they recorded two of their compositions, and released them in the Dumas area on their own record label, the Triple D label called after the local radio station KDDD. The disc was later released commercially on the Blue Moon label, and in late 1956 *Party Doll* by Buddy Knox and the Rhythm Orchids

Buddy Knox, Jimmy Bowen and the Rhythm Orchids, 1957

left to right Jimmy Bowen, Dave Alldred, Buddy Knox, Donnie Lanier

became a big hit in the Dumas area. The record was heard by music publisher Phil Kahl who persuaded the boys to fly to New York and sign for the newly formed Roulette label.

Party Doll was released nationally by Roulette and raced up the American charts to reach number one in the Billboard Hot Hundred on 30 March 1957.

Buddy's second disc, *Rock Your Little Baby To Sleep*, was another big hit. He was in the army doing his national service when this was released (under the name of 'Lieutenant Buddy Knox'), but shortly after was given special leave to fly to New York to play his part in the film *Jamboree*. The number that he sang in this film, *Hula Love*, was his third record and another hit, reaching number thirteen in the Hot Hundred. During the next three years Buddy had several other sizeable hits for Roulette, the biggest being *Somebody Touched Me*.

In 1960 Buddy left Roulette and signed for Liberty Records. His first release for them, *Lovey Dovey*, was a big success, and this was followed by several smaller hits including *She's Gone, Open Your Lovin' Arms, Hitchhike Back To Georgia*. He left Liberty in 1964 and after making one record, *Jo Ann*, for the very small Ruff label in Texas he signed for Reprise in 1965. But though he made some excellent recordings, success eluded him at Reprise.

When he left Reprise in 1967 he decided to go more into the field of country music — this did not involve too radical a change as his work had always had country leanings. In late 1967 he signed for United Artists records in Nashville. So far two records have been released and with the first, *Gypsy Man*, Buddy had a fair-sized hit.

Buddy Knox, Vancouver, Canada, 1969

Brenda Lee

Born Brenda Lee Tarpley on 11 December 1944 in Lithonia, Georgia, and educated at Maplewood School, Nashville.

In 1956 she was heard by country star Red Foley singing in a talent contest in Augusta, Georgia. He was so impressed with her performance that he arranged for her to make her TV debut on 31 March 1956, in the Ozark Jubilee Show. She was such a success that she was asked by major companies to appear

70

Brenda Lee, 1960

on their shows, which led to Decca Records signing her to a long-term contract.

Her first release was the country standard *Jambalaya*, which sold well on a local rather than a national basis. Her first hit came in early 1960 with the beat ballad *Sweet Nothin's*. She appeared on the Perry Como, Dick Clark and Steve Allen shows, her electric stage personality winning new fans. Her next release, *I'm Sorry/That's All You Gotta Do*, won her second gold record and topped the US charts for three weeks.

She came to Britain in 1960 to appear on 'Oh Boy' and amazed everyone with her exciting stage act. She was voted second to Connie Francis as the world's top female vocalist in a poll conducted by one of the leading British pop publications.

Brenda Lee stayed among the leading female vocalists, winning further gold discs in 1962 and 1963.

Leiber and Stoller

Jerry Leiber was born in Baltimore, Maryland, on 25 April 1933. His mother ran a grocery store in a racially mixed neighbourhood, and it was here that the young Jerry became interested in music, after hearing his neighbours singing gospel blues songs on the streets.

Mike Stoller was born in New York City on 13 March 1933. They met while both were students at the City College of Los Angeles, discovered their mutual love of music and decided to try song-writing together. They hit the bigtime in 1956 when *Down In Mexico* became a hit for the Coasters. Later that year they achieved their biggest hit of the year, *Hound Dog*, which went on to notch over five million sales. Further hits came with *Bazoom*, *Black Denim Trousers*, *Love Me*, *Loving You* and *Searchin'*.

They left Los Angeles in 1957 to move to New York, the hub of the music and recording industry, where they continued their successful partnership with *Jailhouse Rock*, *Lucky Lips*, *Yakety Yak*, *King Creole*, *Young Blood* (in collaboration with Jerome 'Doc' Pomus), *Charlie Brown*, etc.

Mike Stoller also appeared in *Jailhouse Rock* with Elvis Presley, playing piano in the *Treat Me Nice* sequence.

They also acted as a producing team for record companies with Mike writing the arrangements and playing piano while Jerry supervised the actual recording.

Today they continue to produce successful compositions although nothing

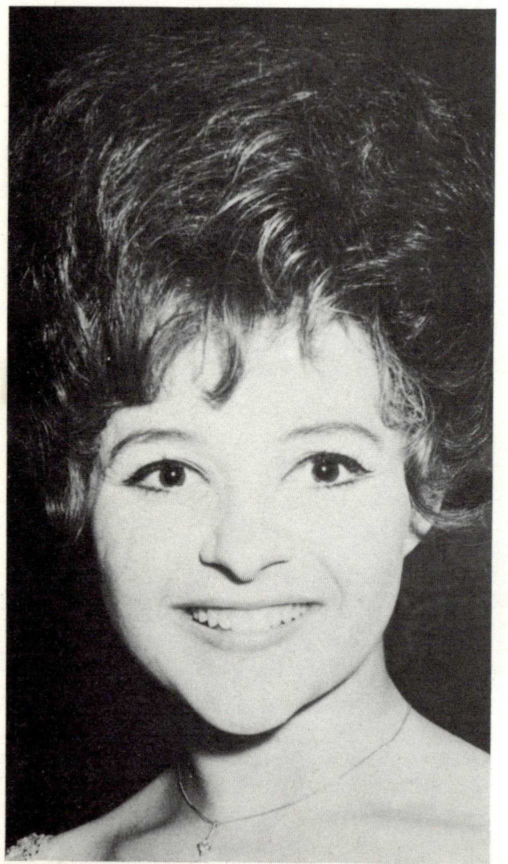

Brenda Lee, 1963

like the number that they turned out in the fifties and early sixties.

Jerry Lee Lewis

Jerry Lee Lewis was born in Feriday, Louisiana on 29 September 1935. His father, Elmo, taught him to play the piano.

It has been reported that when he was eight his parents mortgaged their house to buy him a $900 piano, could not repay and lost their home.

In his early teens he meant to become a minister and attended the Assembly of God Institute in Waxahatchie, Texas.

Eventually, however, he got homesick and returned to Feriday. The harmony and counterpoint he learned while he was playing with the school orchestra came back with him, adding a new dimension to his keyboard work.

He eventually began playing professionally in shows and night clubs, playing mostly gospel material. After hearing how Sam and Judd Phillips had developed Presley into a star he decided to seek an audition with Sun and made his way to Memphis.

Sam Phillips liked his style and his audition tape became his first recording, *Crazy Arms*. He earned his first gold disc with *Whole Lotta Shakin' Goin' On*, recorded in 1957. With his third release, *Great Balls Of Fire/You Win Again* he again made the best sellers, earning his

Jerry Lee Lewis trio in *High School Confidential*, 1958

second gold disc. He appeared in his first film, *Disc Jockey Jamboree*, at this time, making his second appearance in *High School Confidential* (featuring the title tune) the following year.

When he made his first visit to Britain in 1958 there was a storm of criticism from the press over his young bride (she was not quite fourteen) and he cancelled the tour and returned home.

On his return he cut *The Return of Jerry Lee* together with the local DJ George Klein. This was a comedy number with cuts from fourteen Lewis numbers.

He continued to issue such great sides as *Break Up*, *I'll Sail My Ship Alone*, *Lovin' Up A Storm* and *Let's Talk About Us*, each one making the best sellers in many different countries so that Jerry Lee was established as a major international star.

He also cut an instrumental track for Sun subsidiary Phillips International, as the Hawk, *In The Mood/I Get The Blues When It Rains*. Jerry Lee can also be heard backing Carl Perkins on his *Matchbox* recording.

Smiley Lewis

Smiley Lewis was born in Texas and was christened Overton Lemon.

In 1949 he recorded for Deluxe, issuing *Here Comes Smiley/Turn On Your Volume Baby*. Following this release he joined Imperial Records, who were in the process of expanding, and had *Tee-Nah-Nah/Lowdown* issued, followed by *Slide Me Down/Growing Old*. All these titles were recorded in March 1950 with the following personnel: Dave Bartholomew (trumpet), Joe Harris (alto), Salvadore Doucette (piano), Clarence Hall or Lee Allen (tenor), Ernest McLean (guitar), Frank Fields (bass) and Earl Palmer (drums).

His first hit came in 1952 with *The Bells Are Ringing*, other outstanding issues in this early period being *Down The Road* and *Blue Monday* (later recorded by Fats Domino). In late 1955 he recorded *I Hear You Knocking*, with Fats Domino on piano and this became yet another good seller. The following year he recorded *Shame, Shame, Shame* which was featured in the film *Baby Doll*, and must rate among his finest recordings. His last Imperial sides, *Tell Me Who* and *Stormy Monday Blues*, were released in 1960.

After this release nothing was heard until late 1965 when two titles cropped up on Loma, a re-recording of *The Bells Are Ringing* and *Walkin' The Girl*.

Jerry Lee Lewis on stage, 1958

Smiley Lewis was for four or five years one of Imperial's biggest-selling artists. His releases are among the best on the label, not surprisingly as he had the services of an excellent songwriter in Dave Bartholomew and the use of first class musicians, most of whom also worked with Fats Domino.

Frankie Lymon and the Teenagers

Frankie Lymon was born in the tenements of Washington Heights in September 1942. His formative years were spent fighting on the streets and receiving a minimal education at Manhattan's Edwin Stitt School and Quintano's Professional School in New York.

At the age of thirteen he was singing gospel tunes on street corners with four of his class-mates, Sherman Garnes aged fifteen (bass), Joe Negroni aged sixteen (baritone), Herman Santiago aged sixteen (first tenor) and Jimmy Merchant aged fifteen (second tenor).

One summer evening they were seen by Richard Barret who at that time was enjoying a string of big successes as leader of the Valentines. He was to become better known both as a solo performer and from his close connections with the Chantels and the Three Degrees. Richie took the boys to GEE Records, a subsidiary of Roulette, who signed them up.

Their first release in 1956, *Why Do Fools Fall In Love/Please Be Mine*, propelled the group from the poverty-stricken ghettos of Washington Heights into the $8000 a week bracket. The tune remained in the US Hot Hundred for sixteen weeks, topped the UK charts for three weeks and sold some 1,500,000 records all over the world. Frankie wrote

Frankie Lymon and the Teenagers performing in *Mr Rock and Roll*, 1957

the number as a poem when he was in the fifth grade, although the label credits bear a second name. The group left their schooling behind and life for them became a continual whirlwind of TV shows and package tours.

For two years it was impossible to live in the US without hearing of the Teenagers. Many more hits followed on the GEE label, all of which were released by Columbia in the UK. *I Promise To Remember*, *The ABC's Of Love*, *I'm Not A Juvenile Delinquent*, *Teenage Love* and *Miracle In The Rain* all soared up the US Hot Hundred.

Another of Frankie's brothers, Lewis Lymon, formed a group known as the Teenchords, who had minor success with *Honey Honey*, *I'm So Happy* and *Dance Girl* in 1957, also appearing in the film *Disc Jockey Jamboree*.

Frankie's group landed a bit part in *Rock, Rock, Rock* singing *I'm Not A Juvenile Delinquent*. GEE issued an album entitled *The Teenagers* and in the spring of 1957 they came to the London Palladium for a two-week season.

On their return to the US the group split up and Frankie went out as a solo performer moving to Roulette Records.

Until 1961 his solo efforts continued to be released in the UK, all selling in fewer and fewer quantities. By 1961 his singles were no longer issued in the UK and *Jailhouse Rock*, *Change Partners* and *I Put The Bomp* did nothing in America.

At eighteen years of age Frankie was fast becoming washed out and was left to seek a living from the royalties of the tunes he had composed, and as a moderately successful night club entertainer.

Frankie Lymon died in March 1968 from an overdose of drugs, in his grandmother's apartment in New York.

Clyde McPhatter

Clyde was born in the tobacco town of Durham, North Carolina, on 15 November 1933. His father was a preacher at the Mount Calvary Baptist Church and his mother played organ for the services. Together with his brothers Leroy, James and George Jr and sisters Gladys, Esther and Bertha, he sang in the choir there. This early choir singing accounts for the strong gospel feel he was to get in his recordings.

Clyde went to Hillside High School in Durham, and immediately after world war two his family moved to New Jersey where he attended Chelsior High. At fourteen he formed his first vocal group, the Mount Lebanon Singers. They made many public performances, even though all the members were still at school.

On graduation Clyde got a job as a clerk, but continued singing in his spare time. In 1950 he decided to try as a professional and joined Billy Ward's Dominoes as lead tenor. The line-up at the time was Bill Brown (bass), Jimmy van Long (second tenor), Joe Lamont (baritone), Billy Ward and himself. Clyde stayed with the group for three years, appearing on most of their biggest sellers, the most famous of which were *Do Something For Me*, *Harbour Lights*, *When The Swallows Come Back To Capistrano*, *These Foolish Things* and *Have Mercy Baby*.

In 1953 Clyde left the Dominoes (and was replaced by Jackie Wilson). He formed his own band, the Drifters, which signed with Atlantic and recorded their first session in June 1953, in New York. The line-up for that session was Gerhard Thrasher, Billy Pinkney, Charlie Hughes and himself. The initial release was *Money Honey*, which became a hit in many states. During his year with the

Drifters only six other singles, *Lucille, Such A Night, Honey Love, Someday You'll Want Me To Want You, White Christmas* and *Watcha Gonna Do*, were officially made (although many of the singles later released as solos were really Drifters' efforts). Seventeen sides were recorded altogether, the remainder being LP tracks.

He entered the USAF in 1954, joining the Special Services section. While he was serving he managed to cut *Everybody's Laughin'* plus a duet with Ruth Brown, *I've Got To Have You*, the only time he ever teamed with another solo performer on record.

His first real solo release, *Seven Days*, was issued in February 1956 and sold well enough to cause a stir. The follow-up *Treasure Of Love* really established Clyde as a top performer, reaching the US charts and even making the British charts at number twenty-eight. A string of hits followed including *Without Love There Is Nothing*, *Just To Hold My Hand* and *Rock And Cry* (from the film *Mr Rock And Roll*). Clyde at this time made appearances as a bill topper on many big touring shows and appeared in *Mr Rock And Roll*. In December 1958 *A Lover's Question* became Clyde's only million seller, although both *Lovey Dovey* and *Since You've Been Gone* did very well.

In 1959 Clyde signed with MGM, releasing *Bless You* as his initial effort.

In 1960 Clyde visited Britain on the Bobby Darin–Duane Eddy tour, winning new fans with his polished act and promoting his *Think Me A Kiss*. However, none of the six MGM sides released sold as well as his Atlantic efforts and in 1960 Clyde signed with Mercury.

His first single, *Ta Ta*, sold reasonably well, but his biggest sellers came with *I'll Love You Till The Cows Come Home* followed by *Lover Please* which reached number seven in the US Hot Hundred on 17 April 1962. Except for *Little Bitty Pretty One*, he has not enjoyed further chart success although he is still recording and performing club dates regularly.

Johnny Meeks

Johnny is virtually unknown, owing to the fact that 'Galloping' Cliff Gallup is wrongly credited with his work in Gene Vincent's Bluecaps. Cliff Gallup left five or six months after *Be-Bop-A-Lula*, although he is on Vincent's first two albums.

Johnny Meeks was born in 1939 in South Carolina and was, along with Jimmy Burton, one of the first white rock and roll guitarists. Although he was not the best lead guitarist of the fifties some of his lead work, particularly that on *Baby Blue*, was far in advance of most of the lead sounds of the times (except for some of Buddy Holly's solos). He has a very distinct phrasing, sometimes messy, whereby 'strangled' notes are crammed in without respect for timing as in *Summertime* and *Maybelline* (both Gene Vincent, 1958), but certainly producing an interesting result. Johnny also was co-writer of *Say Mama*. After the Bluecaps disbanded Johnny became a much-in-demand session guitarist.

The Moonglows

Bobby Lester, Prentiss Barnes, Alexander Graves and Harvey Fugua formed one of the most popular vocal teams of the fifties, the Moonglows.

Lester and Fugua were born in Louisville and began singing together while they were still in high school, eventually joining Ed Wiley's Band who were at the time touring the Southern States. Harvey Fugua moved to Cleveland in late 1950 where he met Barnes and Graves, both native Clevelanders. They decided to form a group and got Bobby Lester to make it a foursome.

They were heard by Fats Thomas, a Cleveland promoter, who persuaded Alan Freed to audition them. Freed liked their style and signed them to the Champagne label of Cleveland, naming them after his Moondog Show which was a great success at the time.

Champagne folded and they signed with Chance of Chicago, issuing some excellent sides before that too went out of business. Finally they joined Chess, a lucky move which brought them their

first major hit, *Sincerely*. With this first hit they were invited to tour and make the usual promotional appearances on the major TV and radio shows.

They were featured, together with their fifth member (guitarist Billy Johnson) in two rock films, *Mr Rock And Roll* and *Rock, Rock, Rock*, both in 1957. Harvey Fugua was featured as a solo performer in *Go, Johnny, Go* in 1959.

Merrill Moore

Merrill Everett Moore was born in Algona, Iowa, on 26 September 1923.

At eighteen he was playing odd dates and beginning to show promise as a pianist. In 1952 while performing at Jimmy Kennedy's Buckaroo Club in San Diego he was spotted by a scout for

Merrill E. Moore, San Diego, 1969

Capitol Records who eventually signed him to a six-year contract.

Capitol issued the classic *House of Blue Lights* as his initial release and this was an immediate hit.

His television debut was made on the Hometown Jamboree programme with his radio debut coming on the radio version of the show on KXLH. His next release, *Red Lights*, also sold fairly well and soon he found himself touring with such greats as Gene Vincent, Carl Perkins, Johnny Cash and Chet Atkins.

Not only was Merrill himself turning out steady sellers such as *Corina, Corina, Down The Road A Piece* and *Buttermilk Baby*, he was also backing other Capitol acts on their hits, Tommy Sands' *Teenage Crush* and Wanda Jackson's *Party*, among others.

Eventually, though, he left Capitol in September 1958 and began playing clubs in California and Arizona, becoming much in demand as a night club artist.

Merrill Moore was among the first of the keyboard artists to achieve any degree of fame and was quite a prolific recording artist, cutting twenty-eight singles during his contract period.

Rick Nelson

Born Eric Hilliard Nelson in Teaneck, New Jersey on 8 May 1940. His first experience of show business was in 1948 on the radio show The Adventures of Ozzie and Harriet, which featured him together with his parents, Ozzie and Harriet Nelson, and his brother David. He endeared himself to the thousands of listeners and later when the show was transferred to TV he became a firm favourite of the weekly viewers with his

The Moonglows, 1957

catch phrase, 'I don't mess around, boy'.

At the age of sixteen young Ricky branched out on his own as a singer and was immediately accepted by the nation's teenagers. His first release, *I'm Walkin'*, on the Los Angeles based Imperial label, was a million seller, as were his next eight US releases.

He established himself with the British record buyers in 1958 when his version of *Poor Little Fool* entered the top ten. This particular record sold a million copies and earned Ricky a gold disc. A feature of many of Ricky's discs was the brilliant guitar work by James Burton, who has since become much in demand as a session guitarist in the US.

His personal appearances broke box office records everywhere and soon he attracted the attention of many of the larger film companies and was signed for his first major starring role in a Western entitled *Rio Bravo* with John Wayne and Dean Martin. He had previously played himself in *Here Come the Nelsons* and a small part in *A Story Of Three Loves*. He followed *Rio Bravo* with a comedy role with Jack Lemmon in *Wackiest Ship In The Army*.

At this time his records were not having anything like their earlier success so Ricky left Imperial to join US Decca. He broadened his style and recorded many excellent songs without having any success. However, Ricky's earlier show business training stood him in good stead and he was still making regular TV appearances, slowly broadening his style to suit all audiences.

Today Rick (he dropped the 'y' some time ago) is married to starlet Kristin Harmon. He has, with his wife, recently appeared in the film *Love and Kisses* and still records between TV and film appearances.

Ricky Nelson, 1959

Sandy Nelson

Born Sander Nelson on 1 December 1938 in Santa Monica, California. At High School he learned to play the drums and on his graduation joined the local Kip Tyler Band. Eventually he decided to try his hand at obtaining session work in Hollywood, soon becoming a top session man. While sessioning for the Original Sound label in 1959 he was asked if he would record an instrumental he had written, *Teen Beat*. This became one of the best-selling instrumentals, soon reaching a million sales.

In 1960 he signed for Imperial and received his second gold disc for sales of *Let There Be Drums*. By 1961 Sandy had recorded countless best-selling instrumental LPs and had also toured Britain with great success.

The Olympics

Three of the four Olympics were originally in a high school group known as the Challengers and recorded for Melatone Records under that name. Their only release was *I Can Tell/The Mambo Beat*.

The Olympics consisted of Walter Ward (leader and lead singer), born in Jackson, Mississippi; Eddie Frank Lewis (first tenor), born in Houston, Texas; Melvin King (bass), born in Shreveport, Los Angeles; Walter Lee Hammond, the only member not to have been with the Challengers, born in Fort Worth, Texas.

They were spotted performing by two astute talent scouts, John L. Criner and Effie Smith, who renamed them the Olympics and placed them with Demon Records for recording. The result was their initial smash hit *Western Movies*, one of the best novelty hits of 1958.

They followed this with *Dance With The Teacher* and *Big Boy Pete*, neither of which made the impact of their first hit. By 1961 this team had dropped out of sight, having achieved only one really big seller.

Roy Orbison

Roy Kelton Orbison was born on 23 April 1936 in Vernon, Texas. His parents later moved to Wink, Texas, where he attended local school with his elder brother Grady. When Roy was six his father began teaching him to play the guitar.

While in his teens Roy was leader of a group known as the Wink Westerners, comprising: Charles Evans (bass), Billy Parr Ellis (drums), Richard West (piano) and James Morrow (electric mandolin). They played together at local functions, performing mainly country numbers. They eventually landed their own radio programme on KVWC in Vernon, Texas.

Several years later he became friendly with another young Texan, Buddy Holly. Through their meetings Roy and the Teen Kings (his group at the time and consisting of Billy Parr Ellis and James Morrow, and Jack Kennedy, bass guitar, and Johnny 'Peanuts' Wilson, rhythm guitar) travelled to Clovis, New Mexico, to meet Buddy's manager, Norman Petty. He invited them to cut some demo tapes in his studio and two of these led to Roy's first release, *Tryin' To Get To You /Ooby Dooby* on Jewel Records.

In April 1956, Sam Phillips of Sun Records heard a tape of some of Roy's songs, liked them and signed Roy to his label. The result was Sun 242, *Ooby Dooby/Go, Go, Go*. This sold something like 350,000 copies. Three more singles followed for Sun; *You're My Baby*,

Roy Orbison and the Wink Westerners
on stage Jal, New Mexico, 1954

Roy Orbison and the Teen Kings, 1956
left to right Billy Par Ellis, Roy
Orbison, James Morrow, Johnny
Peanuts Wilson, Jack Kennelly

Sweet And Easy and *Chicken Hearted*, none, though, selling anything like the first release.

In 1958 Roy wrote *Claudette*, which was recorded by the Everly Brothers as the B side of their hit *All I Have To Do Is Dream*. The success of this record led to Roy's signing with Wesley Rose, part-owner of Acuff-Rose Publications in Nashville.

Roy next signed for RCA Records but after one release, *Almost Eighteen* and *Jolie*, he left after RCA turned down his demo of *Paper Boy*. Monument Records next signed him and after two releases Roy came up with *Only The Lonely*, which by the summer of 1960 became a number one on both sides of the Atlantic, earning Roy his first gold disc in the process. He followed this up with *Blue Angel*, another mournful ballad, which again reached both the US and English top twenty.

Roy Orbison had steadily gone from strength to strength and is today one of the world's top vocal attractions.

Johnny Otis

Born in Vallejo, California, on 28 December 1921. By his teens he was a capable musician, playing piano, vibes and drums.

By the late 1940s he led his own band and in fact has claimed to have been playing rock and roll then. He first recorded, without any great success, for Peacock and King, but by the late 1950s the Johnny Otis Show was one of the big US teen attractions and had several hits on the Capitol label, such as *Ma, He's Makin' Eyes At Me*, featuring band vocalists Marie Adams and the Three Tons of Joy, and *Willie And The Hand Jive*.

Featured with the band, apart from Marie Adams, were Micki Lynn, Mel Williams and Julie Stevens.

Carl Perkins

Carl Lee Perkins was born in Tiptonville, Tipton County, Tennessee, on 9 April 1932. While in his teens he formed a group with his brothers Jay B. and Clayton (also known as Buck), plus one of his friends on drums.

He eventually auditioned for Sun and signed a contract with them, actually signing on the same day as his friend Johnny Cash.

Carl Perkins on stage, 1956

His first release was on the Sun subsidiary label Flip, *Movie Magg/Turn Around*. His first release on the Sun label was *Let The Juke Box Keep On Playing/Gone, Gone, Gone*.

In 1956 he had his first national hit and million seller, in *Blue Suede Shoes/Honey Don't*. It was recorded on 26 December 1955 and issued the following week on 1 January 1956. Also in 1956 Carl and his brothers plus drummer W. S. Holland appeared in the film *Disc Jockey Jamboree*, singing *Glad All Over*. (The film was not released until 1957, but Carl's part was filmed in 1956.)

Shortly after this while on his way to perform on the Perry Como TV Show he was involved in an accident which killed his manager and seriously injured his brother Jay B. and himself. His brother died in October 1958 after a long illness.

Carl eventually left Sun in 1958, after the release of *Glad All Over* and *Lend Me Your Comb*, to join Columbia.

Carl Perkins is probably one of the finest exponents of the Southern rock-abilly style and certainly, if not for that fateful crash, would have become far more successful on a national basis.

The Platters

Tony Williams, Dave Lynch, Herb Reed, Paul Robi and Zola Taylor formed the Platters, one of the most successful vocal teams of the fifties.

Tony Williams was born in Roselle, New Jersey. He sang in the local church choir and also a number of gospel groups. On leaving high school he enlisted in the USAF and sang with the company band in Kellyfield, Texas. On discharge he decided to try to break into show business and moved to the West Coast, where the business in vocal groups was at an all-time high. While he was working as a car washer in a service station, Buck Ram, a well known talent scout and songwriter, called in and Tony asked him for an audition. Buck was suitably impressed and signed him to a contract. Many months passed before Buck had the idea of forming a vocal group to showcase Tony's talents. First to join was David Lynch from St Louis who became second tenor. David previously drove a cab around Los Angeles and also sang in local night clubs. Baritone Paul Robi, a competent pianist from New Orleans, was signed when he walked into Buck's Personality Productions office for an audition. Zola Taylor, a native of Los Angeles, was picked out of a talent contest. Finally Herbert Reed, from Kansas City, became the group's co-median, a position designed for bass vocalist.

In 1953 the Platters joined Federal Records and recorded a number of tunes which became popular in the local r. and b. market. Some were even issued in the UK on Parlophone: *Beer Barrel Boogie, Voo-Vee-Ah-Bee, Hey Now* and the original version of *Only You*, written by Buck and Ande Rand.

In 1955 Mercury Records signed them for a long-term contract and their initial release, a re-recording of *Only You* (recorded without Zola Taylor) sold a million in the US, reached the top in Britain and sold a million in France. Other big sellers followed with *The Great Pretender, The Magic Touch, My Prayer, You'll Never Know, I'm Sorry, Twilight Time* and *Smoke Gets In Your Eyes*, constituting consistency on a massive scale unequalled by any negro group until the Supremes. The Platters

The Platters, 1957

made their film debut in *Rock Around The Clock* in 1955 and appeared in a string of rock epics including *Rock All Night*, *The Girl Can't Help It* and *Girls' Town*.

In 1960 the Platters visited London and performed on all the top TV shows. They also appeared in South America, the Far East, Europe and Australia that year. However, even with these successful in-person shows behind them, their record sales began to decline, and by 1961 they were no longer the top vocal team, mainly because of their choice of recording material and the change in their line-up (Tony Williams was replaced by Sonny Turner). Nevertheless the Platters will always be remembered for their contribution to the vocal group scene in the rock and roll era.

Elvis Presley

The legendary Elvis Aaron Presley was born in Tupelo, Mississippi, on 8 January 1935. He was one of identical twins, but the other boy did not survive.

His parents were staunch members of a religious order known as the Fundamentalist Assembly of God, and from an early age Elvis was taken to their weekly prayer meetings where he soon came to enjoy the stirring gospel tunes. Their influence is apparent in many of his early recordings.

At twelve he made his first stage appearance singing *Old Shep* in an amateur talent competition at the County Fair in Tupelo.

Shortly after this his parents moved to Memphis and he began to attend Humes High School where he became popular through his impromptu musical sessions held after hours. Eight years later Elvis made a decision which was to lead to his singing career. He was at this time working for the local Crown Electric Company as a truck driver, and one day, while making a delivery, he noticed a sign on a building in Union Avenue advertising recording services. He decided to make a present to his mother of her favourite song, *My Happiness*. When he had recorded *My Happiness*, the engineer told him he was allowed another three songs, so Elvis completed his first (unpaid) recording session with *That's When Your Heartaches Begin*, *Casual Love Affair* and *I'll Never Stand In Your Way*. Sam Phillips, owner of Sun Records, happened to be in the next studio, heard Elvis, and decided to come and see for himself. The result was that for the next eighteen months Sam Phillips spent his time coaching this youngster. Meanwhile, the Presley family were in desperate financial straits as Vernon Presley had to go into hospital leaving Elvis to support his mother and pay his father's medical fees. Then one day while Elvis was in the studios taping some other songs he began playing *That's All Right Mama* during a break for coffee. Immediately the other musicians, Scotty Moore and Bill Black, joined in and Sam Phillips, sensing the excitement created by this great sound ordered an immediate 'take'. A week or so later, after the disc had been given a trial run by three local DJs on their shows, one of the most important discs to be issued on the Sun label, Sun 209, *That's All Right Mama/ Blue Moon Of Kentucky*, was released. It became an immediate hit in the Southern States and soon Elvis was asked to make personal appearances to plug the disc.

In July 1954 Elvis undertook his first big public performance at the Overton Park Shell in Memphis, sharing the bill

Elvis Presley on stage, 1958

Elvis Presley, about 1956

with Slim Whitman, Billy Walker and the Louvin Brothers. At this time he was approached by well known Southern DJ and promoter Bob Neale, who offered his services as manager. Elvis accepted and after hiring drummer D. J. Fontana set out for a tour of the Southern States. Sun Records began issuing further Elvis Presley singles, all big sellers in the South, *Milk Cow Blues, You're A Heartbreaker, Baby Let's Play House,* etc.

Eventually Elvis split with Neale and Scotty Moore acted as his business manager. At the invitation of Hank Snow the boys appeared on Grand Ol' Opry, following that with an appearance on Louisiana Hayride. On this particular show Elvis made a point of featuring his lesser known songs such as *Uncle Penn, Tennessee Saturday Night, Mean Heart Blues* and *Night Train To Memphis,* all of which he is thought to have recorded for Sun, but which are to date unreleased.

Shortly after this, the man who was eventually to shape his career came on the scene. 'Colonel' Tom Parker, a respected figure in the Southern showbiz fraternity, after seeing Elvis perform offered to manage him. Presley was flattered that he should be interested, and accepted the offer. He immediately set to work on making the rest of the US aware of Presley. He reviewed the recording contract and although he was friendly with Sam Phillips, decided that a small Memphis company could hardly be expected to back up the nation-wide promotion he had in mind. The distribution was always a big problem with Sun Records, which was why few of Elvis's early releases ever found their way out of the South.

Parker's problem was soon solved as RCA representative Steve Sholes, whilst passing through Memphis, heard Elvis's *That's All Right* on his car radio, and was so impressed he immediately set out to find this singer with the wild vocal delivery. Eventually Sholes traced Parker and set up a deal for Presley to sign with RCA Records, in the process buying his Sun contract from Sam Phillips for around $35,000, a large sum in those days.

On 10 February 1956 Elvis recorded his first sides for RCA in their Nashville studios, *Heartbreak Hotel/I Was The One.* A few days after the release of these tracks Elvis was invited to appear in the Ed Sullivan Show along with Tommy and Jimmy Dorsey. Naturally he performed both sides of his new release and within days it entered the best-selling lists, reaching number one in a very short time. Elvis had arrived! His next release, *I Want You, I Need You, I Love You* coupled with *My Baby Left Me,* the first disc on which Elvis used a backing group, was also a big seller. With the success of these first two RCA singles behind him Elvis was booked to appear in cabaret in Las Vegas. There he was spotted by film producer Hal Wallis, and signed to appear in *Love Me Tender* (originally *The Reno Brothers*). In Vegas he saw Freddie Bell and the Bellboys do their act and one particular song, *Hound Dog,* stuck in his mind. He decided to include it in his act and also to record it for a possible single. Before his first RCA recording session in New York he discussed *Hound Dog* with Steve Sholes who thought it was a must for recording, so on 2 July 1956 two of his biggest hits, *Hound Dog* and *Don't Be Cruel* were produced. From then on Presley became the biggest thing on the music scene, his films and in-person

appearances playing to capacity audiences. Even when he went into the army on 24 March 1958, he did so with the biggest publicity ballyhoo ever known, and during his two-year army stay records such as *A Fool Such As I* and *Big Hunk O' Love* kept his name in the charts. Today Elvis Presley is still one of the biggest names in show business and will surely be so for a long time to come.

Lloyd Price

Lloyd Price was born on 9 March 1935 in New Orleans into a large musical family. His father was a professional guitarist before becoming a minister and his mother sang and played gospel songs. As Lloyd grew up with his seven brothers and three sisters music was to be heard any time day or night. Every member of the family played one musical instrument or another.

At fourteen Lloyd formed his first group, which played local dates with moderate success. Later when Lloyd attended Kenner High School he began learning to play the trumpet, one of the few instruments not played by any of the family. In his second year at High School his group had become sufficiently competent to obtain a series on Radio WBOK in New Orleans. While he was there he composed *Lawdy Miss Clawdy*, which when played over the air brought an amazing number of requests for more.

Art Rupe of Specialty Records soon arrived on the scene and promptly signed Lloyd and his band to a contract. In late 1951 *Lawdy Miss Clawdy* was issued as their first release and rapidly sold a million. Some excellent tracks were released on Specialty between 1951 and 1957 when he was drafted for service. When he was discharged from the

army Lloyd travelled to Washington where he set up a recording company with two friends, KRC Productions. Lloyd had three releases on this label, *Chicken And The Bop*, *How Many Times* and *Hello Little Girl*. However, because of massive distribution problems they did not sell and eventually Lloyd fixed a deal with ABC Paramount to lease masters to them. His first one, *Stagger Lee*, did the trick and Lloyd soon added a second gold disc to the one he had earned eight years earlier. This was the start of a run of successes with hits coming like *Where Were You (On Our Wedding Day)* and *Personality* (again a million seller) and *I'm Gonna Get Married*, which all sold well overseas as well as in the US. Other US hits at this time included *Won'tcha Come Home/Come Into My Heart*, *Lady Luck/Never Let Me Go*. Appearances on the Dick Clark and Ed Sullivan shows served to consolidate his position as a top attraction, and as singer, co-writer and publisher of three of his big sellers Lloyd earned royalties in excess of half a million dollars. And one thing he did with his money was to establish a grant to help poor negro students pay their way through college.

Eventually, however, his success waned and he found himself overlooked by the majority of the record buyers.

Charlie Rich

Charlie Rich was born in Colt, Arkansas, on 14 December 1934. While he was in high school he performed with a combo and later studied music at the University of Arkansas. He was by this time a good pianist and eventually when he was drafted into the US Air Force he formed his own group, the Velvetones, who were a popular attraction on their base.

Elvis Presley, 1958

Charlie Rich, 1959

After his discharge Charlie went back to cotton farming, and eager to get back into the music business joined Judd Records (Sam Phillips' brother's label) as a session pianist. Bill Justis, who was a regular Phillips' recording artist, heard that Charlie could sing, and after an audition for Sam Phillips Charlie found himself with a contract with the Phillips International label.

His first disc *Whirlwind/Philadelphia Baby* was produced by Bill Justis. His third release, *Lonely Weekends* was a big hit on a national scale, earning Rich star status. This was followed by *Schooldays* and *On My Knees*, both good sellers though more on a regional basis.

Eventually Rich left Phillips around 1961 to join RCA, his initial release being *Big Boss Man*.

Cliff Richard

Born Harry Webb in Lucknow, India on 14 October 1940. His parents brought him to England when he was eight.

On leaving school, he bought a guitar and joined one of the many skiffle groups which were springing up at the time.

He eventually left the group and began singing some evenings at the famous Two I's coffee bar in London's Soho, where so many talented young performers were discovered. He formed his first group while he was there and they called themselves the Drifters. They consisted of Terry Smart (drums), Norman Mitcham (rhythm guitar) and Ian Samwell (lead guitar) with Cliff (or Harry as he was then known) handling the vocals. Shortly before their first out-of-town booking in Nottingham, Norman Mitcham left. They decided not to replace him but to carry on as they were for the time being. Also at this time they chose the name

Cliff Richard for their vocalist, the surname being a dedication to Little Richard.

In the summer of 1958 agent George Ganjou booked the boys on to a Carroll Levis Show at the Gaumont, Shepherds Bush. Levis was so impressed that he asked for a demonstration disc. Very soon Cliff's first (unpaid) recording *Lawdy Miss Clawdy/Great Balls Of Fire*, was in the hands of successful record producer Norrie Paramor, then of EMI Records, who after auditioning Cliff and the Drifters himself signed them to a contract with Columbia (a label within the EMI set-up). Their first recording *Move It/Schoolboy Crush* was issued on 29 August 1958 while they were busy entertaining audiences at one of the Butlin's holiday camps. *Move It* went into the charts and suddenly Cliff found himself in great demand for tours and in-person appearances. His broadcasting debut was made on Saturday Club and first TV appearance on 'Oh Boy' in September 1958.

Cliff and the Drifters were signed to tour with America's Kalin Twins, who had tasted success with *When*, and it was decided that the Drifters would have to expand. Hank Marvin and Bruce Welch were brought in on lead and rhythm guitars respectively, and also to handle any backing vocals, with Ian Samwell switching to bass. Shortly afterwards Ian Samwell left and was replaced by Jet Harris, who had been the Most Brothers' bass guitarist. Tony Meehan (drums) joined around the same time.

Meanwhile Cliff's recording of *High Class Baby* made the best sellers and led to his first film appearance in *Serious Charge* from which came his first million seller, *Livin' Doll*.

In January 1959 he appeared at the

Cliff Richard in *Expresso Bongo*, 1961

New Musical Express Poll Winners'
Concert after winning the new disc
singer award for 1958. He also appeared
in two Royal Command Performances in
1959 and 1960, and had a six-month
season at the London Palladium.

He made his next film appearance
opposite Laurence Harvey in *Expresso
Bongo* and had a hit with one of the tunes,
A Voice In The Wilderness. His following
releases *Please Don't Tease*, *I Love You*
and *Theme For A Dream* were also chart
entries and served to establish Cliff as a
top performer. In 1962 he starred in the
successful musical *The Young Ones*
earning his second gold disc with the
title tune.

In 1960 Cliff and the Shadows (as his
group had renamed themselves) flew to
America for TV and radio appearances
plus a series of one-nighters.

Still a highly successful artist, Cliff
Richard has graduated from being a
Presley imitator to stardom in his own
right.

Little Richard

Born Richard Penniman in Macon,
Georgia, on 25 December 1935. By
fourteen he was singing in his local
church and the following year working
with a medicine show.

In 1951 he won a local talent contest
and eventually landed an RCA recording

Little Richard and his band in *The
Girl Can't Help It*, 1957

contract. His first release under this deal was *Taxi Blues/Every Hour*. This was followed by *Get Rich Quick/Thinkin' About My Mother*. Two releases later he left the label and returned home to join the local Temple Toppers group. They recorded several sides for Peacock including *Fool At The Wheel* and *Little Richard Boogie* (backed by the Johnny Otis Orchestra). Eventually Richard sent a tape to Specialty Records who were sufficiently impressed to reply (one year later) and he landed a solo contract.

His initial Specialty release, *Tutti Frutti* sold over a million as did *Long Tall Sally*, *Rip It Up*, *Lucille*, *Jenny Jenny* and *Keep A Knockin'*, all between 1955 and 1957.

In 1956 he made his film debut in *Don't Knock The Rock*, followed by appearances in *Mr Rock and Roll*, singing *Lucille*, and in *The Girl Can't Help It*, singing the title tune.

In 1958 he entered the Oakwood Adventist College on a two-year course in religion.

When he finally emerged again into show business he signed for End Records cutting *Save Me Lord* and *Milky White Way* as his only singles on that label.

One of the wildest of them all, Little Richard is probably the most exciting visual performer to emerge from the fifties, and even without any big disc success in the sixties could easily fill any theatre with his fans.

Tommy Sands

Tommy Sands was born on 27 August 1937 in Chicago where his father played piano for Ted Lewis while his mother was vocalist with Art Kassell's band.

With his family's musical background

Tommy Sands in a scene from *Sing Boy, Sing*, 1958

it is not surprising that Tommy began singing at nine, broadcasting a couple of times over the local radio station. By twelve he was working after school as a disc jockey in Houston where his family had moved.

In June 1956 Tommy trekked to Hollywood, landing a permanent spot for himself on the Cliffie Stone Hometown Jamboree show. Nine months later he found himself the number one star of the show.

He was signed by Capitol records and his first release, *Teenage Crush*, sold a million in just over six weeks, earning a gold disc. Even before this Tommy had received rave notices for his acting performance on a TV play, *The Singin' Idol*, which led to 20th Century Fox signing him for the film version, *Sing, Boy, Sing*.

His second Capitol release, *Loving You*, helped to further his recording career without selling in any vast quantities.

In 1959 he appeared in *Mardi Gras* with Pat Boone and Gary Crosby. He was at this time continuing to release rather nondescript singles until he finally left Capitol and joined Frank Sinatra's Reprise Records. After several rather unsuccessful Reprise releases he faded into obscurity.

Jack Scott

Born Jack Scafone in Windsor, Ontario, on 24 January 1938. A few years later his parents moved to Detroit, where they brought up their large family (Jack was the eldest of seven children).

At sixteen Jack formed his first band, known as the Southern Drifters, playing mainly country songs. They played regularly at Saturday night functions in the area and were very popular.

While they were at high school in Detroit his friend Leroy Johnson was sent to prison for fighting. Jack wrote a song about this incident and called it *Leroy*. About this period Jack also wrote *My True Love*, dedicating it to a girl friend.

Keen to play professionally, Jack made a demonstration disc of *My True Love/ Leroy* and took it along to record producer Bob Schwartz for his opinion. As the record was playing 'Lucky' Carle, general manager of Southern Music, walked in and listened to the disc, not making any comment. Bob Schwartz thanked Jack for bringing the song and left it there.

The next day Jack received a call from 'Lucky' Carle who asked him if he could take the record to ABC Paramount Records in New York. The outcome was that Jack was offered a contract by Joe Carlton, a. and r. chief of Paramount.

Jack's first disc issued by Paramount was *Two Timin' Woman* coupled with *I Need You Love*, both Scott (the stage surname) compositions. After *Woman* came *Go Wild Little Sadie*, again his own composition. Neither of these first two releases caused much reaction, and when Joe Carlton asked him to join him on the label he was forming Jack accepted, having great faith in Joe's ability as a producer.

Jack's first waxing for Carlton was *My True Love/Leroy* which he had re-recorded. Upon release it became an immediate big seller, reaching a quarter million US sales within two weeks. The disc also registered strongly in Britain, climbing up to the top five. Jack's next Carlton release, *With Your Love/Geraldine*, also registered strongly, putting Jack among 1958's top sellers. *Goodbye*

Jack Scott, 1959

Baby, his third hit, set a record for length of time in the US charts.

In 1959 Jack's Carlton contract was bought by Rank Records of America (Top Rank in the UK) and his first release for them, *What In The World's Come Over You*, became his second million seller. The follow-up to this, *Burning Bridges*, also did well in the US.

In 1961 Jack moved to Capitol Records and made eight releases on this label, only three of which were issued in the UK. None were hits and Jack faded from the recording scene.

Neil Sedaka

Neil Sedaka was born in Brooklyn, New York, on 13 March 1939 and was educated at the local Lincoln High School. He was an outstanding pianist and in fact intended to make a career as a classical pianist. But meanwhile he developed a flair for writing popular music and wrote several tunes used in school productions.

He won a scholarship to the famous Juillard Music School and was chosen by Artur Rubinstein to play on a radio show featuring young talent.

He eventually teamed up with Howard Greenfield and the two had many of their compositions recorded by top stars of the time. Eventually he made a demo disc which he gave to publishers Art Nevins and Don Kirshner, who were more interested in his voice than in the song. Steve Sholes of RCA heard the disc and immediately signed Neil to a contract. *The Diary* was released as his initial offering and became a hit. He won his first gold disc in 1959 with *I Go Ape*, a wild rocker, following it with hits such as *Happy Birthday Sweet Sixteen* and *Breaking Up Is Hard To Do*.

The Shadows

The Shadows, formerly the Drifters, were formed in late 1958 basically as a backing group to Cliff Richard. They consisted of: Terry 'Jet' Harris, Bruce Welch, Hank B. Marvin and Tony Meehan.

Jet Harris (bass guitar) was born on 6 July 1939 in Kingsbury, London. He earned his nickname through his prowess as a sprinter at school. With the coming of the skiffle craze Jet was asked by leader Wally Whyton to join the Vipers. After leaving them he backed the Most Brothers for a while before eventually joining Tony Crombie's Rockets.

Hank Marvin (lead guitar) was born in Newcastle on 28 October 1941. He became interested in music at fifteen when he bought a banjo from a school-master. He later switched his interest to guitar. Bruce Welch (rhythm guitar) was born at Bognor Regis, Dorset, on 2 November 1941, and moved to New-castle with his parents six months later. While they were at school Hank and Bruce played together in a group known as the Railroaders. In April 1958 the two went to London, joined a group called the Five Chesternuts and recorded *Teenage Love/Jean Dorothy*.

Tony Meehan (drums) was born in Hampstead, London, on 2 March 1943. At thirteen he joined his first dance band and also played tympani with the London Youth Orchestra. After playing in cabaret bands in London's Churchill and Stork clubs he eventually joined Jet Harris in the Vipers.

The four joined up as a group when Cliff Richard was asked to tour with the US act the Kalin Twins and hired them to back him for the tour. At that time they were known as the Drifters but after their first recording for EMI's Columbia label, *Feelin' Fine/Don't Be A Fool With Love*, was released in the States there was a name clash with the US team the Drifters and they had to change their name to the Shadows, a name chosen by Jet Harris.

After the tour Cliff asked them to stay on as permanent backing group. They agreed and appeared with him in *Expresso Bongo*, and the Royal Variety Shows in 1959 and 1960, plus a six-month season at the London Palladium.

In July 1960 they achieved their first number one with *Apache*, winning a silver disc for sales exceeding 250,000. They followed this with hits such as *Man Of Mystery* and *F.B.I.*, earning the title of Top British Small Group in a nation-wide poll.

Today the Shadows have disbanded but must rank as the top British instrumental unit of the late fifties and the sixties.

Huey Smith and the Clowns

Huey 'Piano' Smith was born in New Orleans on 26 January 1934. After leaving school he joined a recording studio as an engineer. He finally decided to make a living as a professional musician and formed his own band, the Clowns. He signed with Ace Records and in 1957 cut *Rockin' Pneumonia And The Boogie Woogie Flu* which swiftly became a smash hit and earned his first gold disc.

In fact Smith did not sing the lead vocals, that job went to Frankie Ford and Bobby Marchan.

The Shadows recording, 1960

Warren Smith, 1958

Warren Smith

Warren Smith was born in Mississippi around 1940. His early years were spent listening to his country favourites on the Grand Ol' Opry and learning to play guitar. His family moved to Memphis where he completed his education at the local high school.

He left school in 1956 and went to Sam Phillips for an audition. He was accepted and signed to a contract. His first disc *Rock And Roll Ruby* was written by Johnny Cash and sold very well.

His follow-up *Black Jack David* also did well and established Warren as a star.

Other releases of note were *Miss Froggie, I've Got Love If You Want It* and *Sweet Sweet Girl* (which was his final Sun single).

In 1959 he left Sun and Memphis and moved to the West Coast.

He became interested in country music and toured there with many top names. He landed a contract with Liberty and released *Odds And Ends*, which became a minor hit.

Tommy Steele

Born Tommy Hicks on 17 December 1936 in the Bermondsey district of South London. At fifteen he joined the Merchant Navy and stayed at sea for four and a half years.

While on leave in 1956 he formed a group called the Cavemen which broke up when Tommy had to return to sea.

Finally Tommy decided to leave the sea and try for professional recognition as a singer. He was spotted singing in Soho's Two I's Coffee Bar and signed to a contract by manager John Kennedy. A Decca recording contract was negotiated and his first single issued shortly afterwards, *Rock With The Caveman/Rock Around The Town*. It leapt into the charts and led to his first appearance at the Empire Theatre, Sunderland.

He made his first appearance in films with Pat O'Brien in *Kill Me Tomorrow*. His first big hit came in 1957 with *Singing The Blues* and he also made two further film appearances in *The Tommy Steele Story* and *The Duke Wore Jeans*. Further hits followed with *Handful Of Songs* and *Tallahassee Lassie*, establishing Tommy as the top British rock performer. In 1957 he was included in the Royal Variety Performance and in 1958 appeared at the London Coliseum and also went on to star in the film *Tommy The Toreador*.

By the 1960s Tommy Steele had drifted away from his rock beginnings and matured into an international star.

Tommy Steele recording *Rock With the Caveman*, 1957

Tommy Steele in *Kill Me Tomorrow*, 1956

Sun Records

Sam C. Phillips, disc jockey, promoter and lawyer, was the man responsible for setting up Sun Records, the small but influential Memphis label.

For most rockabilly fans the story begins with Sun 209, *That's All Right Mama*, recorded by a young Memphis truck driver, Elvis Presley. Slowly Phillips began signing and recording some of the finest rockabilly talent around, including such names as Carl Perkins, Jerry Lee Lewis, Johnny Cash, Roy Orbison, Warren Smith, Charlie Feathers and Billy Riley.

Sun Records was formed around 1950 when Phillips began recording blues artists, leasing the tracks to Modern/RPM and Chess labels. In these early days items by Doctor Ross, James Cotton, Jimmy and Walter, among others, cropped up in the catalogue. There were also a number of non-blues artists such as Earl Peterson, Dusty Brooks and Harmonica Frank.

During the Presley era many of the artists would play on each other's sessions, for example, Roy Orbison is the lead guitarist on Jerry Lee's *Whole Lotta Shakin'*. This co-operation led to some great discs and also created arguments amongst collectors as to who actually appears as backing musicians on some titles. For instance, Elvis Presley is *not* the guitarist on the Billy Emerson *No Greater Love* record.

Apart from the artists appearing on the Sun label, Sam Phillips is said to have recorded Buddy Holly, Sam Cooke, the Everly Brothers, Conway Twitty and Eddie Cochran, but never released any of their material. The following titles by Roy Orbison were also recorded but never issued, *So Long, I'm Gone, I Was A Fool, You Tell Me, Never Let Me Go, You've Got Love, An Empty Cup* and *I've Had It.*

After Presley's contract had been bought by RCA, Phillips concentrated his efforts mainly on Carl Perkins and Johnny Cash. Both of these artists gained gold records, displaying Phillips' sound knowledge of the commercial market. It should be noted that Sun's recording techniques were undoubtedly the most advanced of their time, as careful listening to any track will prove.

Vernon Taylor

Vernon Taylor was born on 9 November 1937 in Sandy Spring, Maryland. During his youth his family was constantly on the move as his father, who was a farmer, moved from place to place seeking work.

In 1948 his father gave up farming and the family moved to Spencerville, Maryland. Vernon became interested in music and having already learned to play the guitar began playing and singing whenever he could find an audience. In 1952 he graduated from Sherwood High School and formed his first band, playing for local parties and dances.

By eighteen he was playing several times a week and had his own show on the local radio station. He got his big break while appearing on a show in Glen Echo, Maryland in July 1957, together with the country star Mac Wiseman. Mac had then just been appointed Recording Manager for DOT Records and after hearing Vernon perform signed him to a contract. Three days after Vernon recorded his first DOT release *Losing Game/I've Got The Blues*, accompanied by the Jordanaires. Neither this nor any of the subsequent DOT releases caused much reaction and he eventually joined Sun.

Vernon Taylor, 1959

His first Sun session produced *Breeze/ Today Is A Blue Day*, which was followed by *Mystery Train/Sweet And Easy To Love*. None of the Sun releases caused much of a stir either, and Taylor faded from the recording scene.

Conway Twitty

Born Harold Jenkins in Friars Point, Mississippi, on 1 September 1933.

His father gave him a guitar when he was five and Harold quickly learned the rudiments of playing. Before long the father and son team was a popular attraction at get-togethers. At ten Harold performed on the local radio station.

While he was in his teens the family moved to Helena, Arkansas, where he went to the local high school. By thirteen he had organized his own band, the Phillips County Ramblers, who became

so popular that they were given their own local radio show. In 1954 he joined the army and was eventually posted to the Far East. He formed a combo from army friends and they were known as the Cimarrons. They won numerous service talent competitions and these led to their own radio series in Tokyo, Japan.

He completed his service in 1956 and had to decide between a career as a professional baseball player (he was outstanding at the sport) or an attempt to make the big time as a singer. Fortunately he chose to try singing, and he won himself a spot on Tabby West's Ozark Jubilee Show.

He approached Sam Phillips of Sun Records with a view to obtaining the much needed recording contract, and although he was turned down he recorded a demo of a song he had written with Roy Orbison, *Rockhouse*, coupled with *You're My Baby*.

The following year, 1957, he acquired a personal manager named Don Seat, who was responsible for changing his name from Jenkins to the unforgettable 'Conway Twitty'.

Conway Twitty was launched and Seat quickly arranged a recording contract with Mercury Records. Conway had stockpiled a large number of his compositions ready for his record debut and only a few were used during his short (six-record) stay with Mercury. The following represent his total output with Mercury: *Born To Sing The Blues, Maybe Baby, Shake It Up, I Need Your Lovin', Double Talk* and *Why Can't I Get Through To You*. None were vast sellers and he had to wait until September 1958, when his five-year MGM contract was signed, before he experienced recording success. For his first recording,

MGM chose a song Twitty had written with drummer Jack Nance in just seven minutes, *It's Only Make Believe*. The choice proved correct as in a few weeks the disc had rocketed into the Hot Hundred both in the US and many other parts of the world. He visited Britain in May 1959 for a spot on the 'Oh Boy' show, returning again in May 1960, after having hits with *Story Of My Love, Mona Lisa, Danny Boy* and *Lonely Blue Boy*. His line-up at the time was Jack Nance (drums), Joe E. Lewis (bass) and Al Brunneax (lead guitar).

After a successful screen test Conway landed parts in *Platignum High School, College Confidential* and *Sex Kitten Goes To College*. He also wrote the title music for all three films.

Apart from using his own group MGM augmented the sound on Twitty's records by using either Grady Martin or Hank Garland as lead guitarist. And the Jordanaires, well known as the backing on many Presley recordings, are also featured on many of Twitty's recordings, dating from *It's Only Make Believe*.

Ritchie Valens

Born Richard Valenzuela in Pacoima, California, on 13 May 1941. He took to the guitar from an early age and by the time he had reached his teens had become highly proficient.

At seventeen he signed for Del-Fi Records of Hollywood and with his first offering *Come On, Let's Go*, entered the US charts.

His second release, *Donna/La Bamba*, sold over a million, earning him his only gold disc. Shortly before leaving to tour in the 'Winter Dance Party' package he completed his first and only film part in Hal Roach Jr's *Go, Johnny, Go*.

Conway Twitty and Joe Lewis on stage, Wembley 1969

His final appearance was made at the Surf Ballroom in Clear Lake, Iowa, together with Dion and the Belmonts, Frankie Sardo, the Crickets, Buddy Holly and the Big Bopper. Together with Holly and the Bopper he decided to fly to their next venue in Fargo, North Dakota.

A snow storm blew up as they were taking off. The plane crashed in a field on the Albert Juhl farm, fifteen miles northwest of Mason City, Iowa, and all the passengers were killed.

Although he made comparatively few recordings it was obvious that Valens was a person of rare talent and had he lived he would surely have been one of the top artists in the US.

The Ventures

Don Wilson, Bob Bogle, Nokie Edwards (lead, bass and rhythm guitars) and Howie Johnson (drums).

The Ventures, 1960
left to right Don Wilson, Nokie
Edwards, Howie Johnson, Bob Bogle

Ritchie Valens, 1959

Don Wilson and Bob Bogle met while working in the building trade. They later teamed up with Nokie and Howard to form a group.

After working at several bookings they eventually formed their own record label, Blue Horizon Records, cut *Walk, Don't Run* and sent copies to the major disc jockeys.

They eventually signed for Dolton Records and sold a million when *Walk, Don't Run* was released nationally in 1960.

They continued to turn out records until the next year they earned their second gold disc with *Perfidia*.

Their output of instrumental releases is still prolific and to date they are easily the most successful small instrumental combo still recording.

Gene Vincent

Vincent Eugene Craddock was born at Munden Point, Norfolk, Virginia, on 11 February 1935. He was educated at South Norfolk High and at this period was particularly interested in the blues.

At fifteen Gene lied about his age to join the US Navy, and after seeing most of the western world during his basic training, was finally sent on active duty in Korea.

Gene Vincent and the Bluecaps in *Hot Rod Gang*, 1959

In 1953 his left leg was severely injured in a motorcycle accident. He spent the next twelve months in a US Navy hospital in Japan before being sent back home to the States. In mid 1954 he was demobilized and entered civilian life, with a shattered leg in a half cast and two Distinguished Service Medals.

He had done a fair amount of singing while he was in the services, mostly informal get-togethers with service friends, and on his discharge decided to try professionally. He began to get spots on local radio stations and in 1956 met Sheriff Tex Davis, a popular local DJ, who was sufficiently impressed with Gene's voice to arrange for him to appear on Country Showtime, the c. and w. spot on WCMS.

In March 1956 he got together with Tex Davis and the two composed *Be-Bop-A-Lula*, destined to become one of the great standard rock compositions. A demonstration disc was cut of *Lula* and submitted to Ken Nelson of Capitol Records, who were desperately searching at the time for an answer to Presley. Nelson, after listening to the demo, signed Gene to a long-term contract, issuing *Be-Bop-A-Lula* as the first release. By late 1956 the disc was a national hit and Gene and his group the Bluecaps

Gene Vincent on stage, London 1960

among Capitol's hottest properties. Gene made his first film appearance at this time in *The Girl Can't Help It*, singing *Be-Bop-A-Lula*.

In 1957, together with Little Richard and Eddie Cochran, Gene toured Australia on a package tour which was so successful that Gene was asked to appear in New Zealand the following year together with Johnny Cash. When the Bluecaps finally disbanded, Gene teamed up with guitarist Jerry Merritt (the guitarist on the *Crazy Times* album), a friend of long standing, and embarked on an extremely successful tour of Japan.

In November 1959 Gene arrived in Europe for his first visit, and made his UK debut at the Tooting Granada as a guest on the Marty Wilde Show. His performance was sensational and immediately Granada signed him for a series of twelve one-nighters. The booking was extended and in late January 1960 he was joined by his friend Eddie Cochran. The two were the stars of a mammoth rock package show which toured Britain. This ended tragically on 17 April 1960 when Eddie was killed and Gene badly injured in a car accident in Wiltshire. After recovering from his injuries Gene continued to tour, wearing the black leather outfit that was to become his trademark. He eventually settled for a while in England where he became a popular part of the music scene. Today Gene is still a popular star among the

Boy Meets Girls group picture, 1960
left to right Billy Fury, Jess Conrad, Gene Vincent, Joe Brown, Eddie Cochran, Adam Faith, Marty Wilde

rock fans and continues to record, although now he veers more towards country music.

Johnny 'Guitar' Watson

Johnny Watson was born in Houston, Texas, on 3 February 1937. Johnny's first guitar was a gift from his grandmother, and he set about learning to play the blues using first-hand knowledge he had picked up from such 'greats' as Lowell Fulsom and T-bone Walker. When his parents separated in 1950 Johnny moved to Los Angeles with his father, and continued his schooling at Jefferson High. He entered and won many local talent contests which quickly brought him to the notice of the local musicians.

On leaving college he joined the Chuck Higgins Band and became a popular attraction while he was with them. He later moved on to play with the Joe Houston and Jay McNeely outfits who appeared at many of the top Los Angeles night spots and eventually became so popular that he decided to form his own band, the line-up being Jason Hogan (baritone), Gaynell Hodge (piano), Milton Bradford (tenor), Ralph Watson (bass) and Charles Prendergraft (drums).

In 1953 he was spotted with his band by local DJ Hunter Hancock who gave them an introduction to the local Federal Records, Johnny was signed and was

Larry Williams and Johnny 'Guitar' Watson, London 1964

accompanied on his first session by the Amos Milburn band, the result being *Highway 60*, which did reasonably well locally, as did the follow-up *Motor Head Baby*. The record company released all of the Federal material under the name of Young John Watson.

He next signed for RPM. His first two releases for them, *Hot Little Mama* and *Too Tired* did not exactly cause wide reaction saleswise but *Those Lonely, Lonely Nights* became a hit. He began touring and was gaining a big reputation as a guitarist when he decided that as well as recording himself he would play for other recording performers. Apart from Larry Williams, whom Johnny was to meet later in his career, he recorded with the Olympics, Eugene Church and the Robins. At this period he was also recording regularly himself and had releases available on no less than three labels, Keen, Class and Goth.

He finally returned to King (a label under the Federal banner) in July 1961 where he released *Embraceable You* as his comeback offering. He also recorded three sides with the Johnny Otis Orchestra, *In The Evenin'*, *Gangster of Love* and *These Lonely, Lonely Feelings*.

Johnny Watson has since gone from strength to strength both as a guitarist working with Larry Williams and as a solo performer in his own right.

Thomas Wayne

Thomas Wayne was born in Memphis, Tennessee, on 22 July 1940 and was christened Thomas Perkins. Both he and his brother Luther (later to become famous as Johnny Cash's guitarist) were interested in music from early days, both learning guitar and Thomas in addition learning to play the piano.

Eventually he signed with Mercury Records cutting *You're The One That Done It* and *This Time*. Neither created much demand and he eventually left Mercury and moved to Fernwood, a small label.

It was a wise move and resulted in a gold disc for *Tragedy*, his initial release. He was at this time managed by Scotty Moore, Presley's guitarist, who also played on the *Tragedy* session.

His follow-up disc, *Eternally*, did not register and he slipped out of the public eye. He also had one release on Phillips International, *I've Got It Made/The Quiet Look*.

Bert Weedon

Born in East Ham, London on 10 May 1920. He was twelve when he received his first guitar and he began seriously studying with a view to playing professionally.

During his early days in show business Bert played with many of the top bands of the time including Ted Heath, Mantovani and Ronnie Aldrich. He soon landed himself a residency as featured soloist on the BBC's show band, which meant broadcasting three times a week on the country's top dance music show.

With the coming of rock and roll Bert was soon in demand and was the unnamed soloist on early records by, among others, Tommy Steele, Cliff Richard, Adam Faith and Frankie Vaughan.

In 1959, by this time signed as a solo performer, Bert waxed the memorable *Guitar Boogie Shuffle* for Top Rank Records, and this became the first disc by a solo British guitarist to reach the charts. Further hits followed with *Nashville Boogie*, *Ginchy*, *Sorry Robbie* and *Some Other Love*. With these hit records

behind him Bert found himself much in demand as a solo attraction on many of the top TV and radio shows.

On nine occasions Bert has been voted Britain's top guitarist in national popularity polls, a position which he enjoys today.

Marty Wilde

Marty Wilde was born Reginald Leonard Smith in Greenwich, London, on 15 April 1939.

In 1958 he was spotted by impresario Larry Parnes in London's Condor Club, and was signed to a management contract. Parnes gave him a new name and a new wardrobe and booked him into the plush Winston's Club where Josephine Douglas, TV personality and producer of the popular Six-Five Special show, saw him and booked him for a spot.

Noted recording producer Johnny Franz, of Phillips Records, liked what he heard and within a few days had signed Marty to a lucrative contract. His debut single was *Honeycomb*, a 'cover' of a US hit, which did not set the charts on fire. His first hit came with *Endless Sleep* and was followed by *Donna* and *A Teenager In Love*. He began touring with his group, the Wild Cats, and was voted number two British singer in 1958. He made his film debut in *Jet Storm*, with Richard Attenborough, Stanley Baker and Mai Zetterling.

The following year he was one of the

Billy Fury and Marty Wilde in Boy Meets Girls, 1960

stars of Jack Good's 'Oh Boy' show together with Cliff Richard and Vince Eager.

By late 1960, however, Marty's popularity with the record buyers had waned, although his live appearances still continued to be successful.

Larry Williams
(see illustration page 112)

Larry Williams was born in New Orleans on 10 May 1935. When Larry was two his parents left New Orleans and moved to Oakland, California. During this period of upheaval Larry was sent to stay with an aunt in Chicago and he was ten when he rejoined his parents in Oakland.

In 1951, when he was sixteen, Larry became friendly with a boy called Oscar Monroc who was at the time leading a small group known as the Teardrops. Larry joined the group playing bass, an instrument on which he was fairly proficient, although he was by this time beginning to take an interest in the piano. Oscar agreed to teach Larry how to play the piano and soon found that Larry had great natural ability on the instrument. Then disaster struck. Because of a slight disagreement within the band Larry refused to travel to a booking in Reno, Nevada; so the others, Oscar, Terry Carter, James Moody and a lad named Brice carried on to the booking without him. On the way home the car turned over and Oscar and Terry were killed. Without Oscar as leader the Teardrops disbanded and Larry found himself out of a job.

In the YMCA club in Oakland, one day, Larry saw a group of local boys practising and being impressed with their sound asked if they would like to join him in forming a new group. The boys agreed and after a few weeks' rehearsal took to the road as the Lemondrops. They played at various local functions performing tunes by Fats Domino, Lloyd Price and Ray Charles. They began to make a big impact locally, drawing crowds wherever they appeared.

In 1954 the band split up and Larry began touring, visiting many of the West Coast clubs, and sitting in with some of the better known groups and singers. In this way he met singer/guitarist Pee Wee Kingsley, later to become the husband of Sugar Pie Desanto. They became friends and Larry played with Pee Wee's band on and off for short periods, but as he could not play regularly with the band Larry decided to move on.

Then in early 1955, while on a visit to his home town he met Lloyd Price, and the two formed a band. Lloyd was at the time on leave from the army but did not return as he wanted to spend more time with the band. Unfortunately for him the military police soon caught up with him and he was sent for trial charged with being absent without leave. Lloyd was found guilty and sentenced to seventeen months' imprisonment. Larry was not well known enough to hold the band together in his own name and so it disbanded with Larry returning to New Orleans.

Larry met there Fats Domino who offered him a job in his band. Although there was no chance of playing the piano Larry needed the work so he joined. This was to prove an excellent move in the long run, as in later years many people he met through being with Fats were able to help his solo career. On account of bad financial problems Larry was forced to leave the band and returned to Oakland. His next job was in a local textile factory working alongside Pee Wee Kingsley, but no sooner was he settled than he got the sack.

He went then to Hollywood. After borrowing money to get there Larry made his way to Specialty Records where he managed to see Art Rupe, who owned the label. Rupe heard him sing and decided he would give him a chance. The following day Larry received a call from Bumps Blackwell, the a. and r. man, who asked him to rush to the studio to record a song that was breaking big for Lloyd Price.

Larry's first sides for Specialty were *Just Because* and *Let Me Tell You Baby*, the line-up being Larry (vocals), Plas Johnson (tenor), Alvin 'Red' Ryler (baritone), Ernie Freeman (piano), Renee Hall and Barney Kessell (guitars), Ted Brinson (fender bass), Ray Brown (string bass) and Earl Palmer (drums). This line-up, except for Ernie Freeman (Larry later did his own piano work) and Gerald Wilson (trumpet), was present at most of his Specialty sessions.

On issue *Just Because* sold well enough for Specialty to sign Larry to a two-year contract. Other hits followed in 1957 with *Short Fat Fanny* and *Bony Maronie* and Larry soon became a firm favourite with audiences all over the world.

Otis Williams and the Charms

Otis Williams was born into a musical family and attended the Woodrow Wilson High School in Cincinnati, Ohio.

The Charms consisted of Roland Bradley, Joe Penn, Richard Parker and Donald Peak. They met up with Otis while they were still in school, and performed at parties and school dances.

In 1954 they signed with King and had their first releases on the DeLuxe subsidiary. *Hearts Of Stone* became their first hit and went on to sell a million in 1955. Other hits followed with *Crazy, Crazy Love, Mambo Sh-Mambo, Ling Ting Tong* and *Ivory Tower*. Between 1958 and 1964 the Charms' records were issued on the parent King label with *The Secret, Just Forget About Me, Panic, When We Get Together* and *Two Hearts* achieving hit status. Their last King release was *Unchain My Heart*.

Otis Williams and the Charms were slightly different from most of the other black vocal teams in that many of their releases were not just rock ballads but had also some fine up-tempo material.

Jackie Wilson

Born in Detroit, Michigan, on 9 June 1936. He graduated from Highland Park School in 1952 and the following year joined Billy Ward's Dominoes as lead voice, taking over from Clyde McPhatter. In 1952 he had also won the Golden Gloves welterweight championship claiming to be eighteen — had he given his real age he would have been ineligible.

In 1957 Jackie decided he would try to make it as a solo performer and signed a management contract with Nat Tarnpol, a Detroit music publisher. He was then signed to Brunswick and had *Reet Petite* issued as his debut single. It did very well, making both the US and UK charts.

In 1959 he won his first gold disc with *Lonely Teardrops*, a dynamic beat ballad. His stage act about this time was getting rave reviews in the music press.

Other big sellers came with *That's Why, Night,* and *Doggin' Around, Night* winning his second gold disc.

He also appeared in two films, *Go, Johnny, Go* and *Teenage Millionaire*.

Jackie Wilson, 1959

17 GREAT RECORDING STARS!
21 BIG HIT TUNES!
YOUR 19 TOP DISK-JOCKEY FAVORITES ARE ALL IN WARNER BROS.' GREAT BIG

A fast-spinning love story behind the scenes of today's brand new kind of Tin Pan Alley!

JAMBOREE

Fats Domino! "Wait and See"

Jerry Lee Lewis! "Great Balls of Fire"

Buddy Knox! "Hula Love"

Jimmy Bowen! "Cross Over"

Charlie Gracie! "Cool Baby"

The Four Coins! "Broken Promise"

The great COUNT BASIE BAND with JOE WILLIAMS

featuring JODIE SANDS · CARL PERKINS · SLIM WHITMAN
LEWIS LYMON & THE TEENCHORDS · RON COBY · CONNIE FRANCIS
ANDY MARTIN · ROCCO & HIS SAINTS · FRANKIE AVALON

—and all these smash tunes too! JAMBOREE · GLAD ALL OVER · FOR CHILDREN OF ALL AGES · TOREADOR · RECORD HOP NIGHT · WHO ARE WE TO SAY · TEACHER'S PET · SAYONARA · SIEMPRE · YOUR LAST CHANCE · IF NOT FOR YOU · UNCHAIN MY HEART · ONE O'CLOCK JUMP · I DON'T LIKE YOU NO MORE · TWENTY FOUR HOURS A DAY

Screen Play by **LEONARD KANTOR** · Directed by **ROY LOCKWOOD** · Produced by **MAX J. ROSENBERG & MILTON SUBOTSKY**

Major US films featuring rock performers, 1955–61

Rock Around The Clock (Columbia 1955) Bill Haley and the Comets, Tony Martinez and his Band, Freddie Bell and the Bellboys, Alan Freed, the Platters.

Love Me Tender (Fox 1956) Elvis Presley.

Don't Knock The Rock (Columbia 1956) Bill Haley and the Comets, Alan Dale, Alan Freed, the Treniers, Dave Appell and the Applejacks, Little Richard.

The Girl Can't Help It (Fox 1957) Little Richard, Eddie Cochran, Gene Vincent, Fats Domino, the Platters, Eddie Fontaine, the Treniers, the Three Chuckles, Johnny Olenn, Abbey Lincoln, Ray Anthony And His Band, Julie London.

Mr Rock And Roll (Paramount 1957) Little Richard, Chuck Berry, Alan Freed, Brook Benton, Teddy Randazzo, Moonglows, Clyde McPhatter, Frankie Lymon and the Teenagers, Lavern Baker, Teddy Randazzo, Ferlin Husky, Lionel Hampton.

Jailhouse Rock (MGM 1957) Elvis Presley.

Disc Jockey Jamboree (Warners 1957) Fats Domino, Jerry Lee Lewis, Buddy Knox, Carl Perkins, Jimmy Bowen, Frankie Avalon, Lewis Lymon and the Teenchords, Connie Francis, Charlie Gracie, Joe Williams.

Rock All Night (Anglo-Amalgamated 1957) the Platters, the Blockbusters.

Untamed Youth (Warners 1957) Eddie Cochran, the Hollywood Rock And Rollers.

Rock, Rock, Rock (Warners 1957) Chuck Berry, the Johnny Burnette Trio, Alan Freed, Frankie Lymon and the Teenagers, the Moonglows, the Flamingos, Lavern Baker.

Loving You (Paramount 1957) Elvis Presley.

The Big Beat (Universal International 1958) Fats Domino, the Diamonds, the Four Aces, the Del-Vikings, the Lancers, etc.

Rock Baby, Rock It (J. G. Tiger Production 1958) Johnny Carroll, Roscoe Gordon.

High School Confidential (MGM 1958) Jerry Lee Lewis, Ray Anthony.

Sing Boy, Sing (Twentieth Century Fox 1958) Tommy Sands.

Let's Rock (Columbia 1958) Paul Anka, Danny and the Juniors, Roy Hamilton, Royal Teens, Della Reese, Tyrones, Julius La Rosa, Wink Martindale.

King Creole (Paramount 1958) Elvis Presley.

Hot Rod Gang, (alternate title *Fury Unleashed*) (Anglo-Amalgamated 1959) Gene Vincent and the Bluecaps.

Go, Johnny, Go (Valiant 1959) Eddie Cochran, Chuck Berry, Ritchie Valens, Alan Freed, Jimmy Clanton, the Cadillacs, the Flamingos, Jackie Wilson, Harvey of the Moonglows.

Juke Box Rhythm (Columbia 1959) Johnny Otis, the Nitwits, Jack Jones, Earl Grant Trio.

Because They're Young (Columbia 1960) Duane Eddy and the Rebels, Dick Clark.

G.I. Blues (Paramount 1960) Elvis Presley.

Teenage Millionaire (United Artists 1961) Jimmy Clanton, Bill Black's Combo, Dion, Marv Johnson, Chubby Checker.

A listing of million sellers by rock artists 1955–1961

Records released before 1961 but which did not achieve a million sales until after that date, are omitted from this list.

		US Label	UK Label	Date
Diana	Paul Anka	ABC Paramount	Columbia	1957
You Are My Destiny	Paul Anka	ABC Paramount	Columbia	1958
Put Your Head On My Shoulder	Paul Anka	ABC Paramount	Columbia	1959
Puppy Love	Paul Anka	ABC Paramount	Columbia	1960
My Home Town	Paul Anka	ABC Paramount	Columbia	1960
Lonely Boy	Paul Anka	ABC Paramount	Columbia	1960
Tears On My Pillow	Little Anthony	End	HMV	1958
Dede Dinah	Frankie Avalon	Chancellor	HMV	1957
Just Ask Your Heart	Frankie Avalon	Chancellor	HMV	1958
Why	Frankie Avalon	Chancellor	HMV	1958
Venus	Frankie Avalon	Chancellor	HMV	1958
Tweedle Dee	Lavern Baker	Atlantic	London	1955
Jim Dandy	Lavern Baker	Atlantic	London	1957
I Cried A Tear	Lavern Baker	Atlantic	London-American	1959
The Twist	Hank Ballard	King	Columbia	1960
Finger Poppin' Time	Hank Ballard	King	Columbia	1960
Maybelline	Chuck Berry	Chess	London	1955
Roll Over Beethoven	Chuck Berry	Chess	London	1955
School Day	Chuck Berry	Chess	Columbia	1956
Rock and Roll Music	Chuck Berry	Chess	London	1957
Sweet Little Sixteen	Chuck Berry	Chess	London	1958
Johnny B. Goode	Chuck Berry	Chess	London	1958
Smokie	Bill Black Combo	Hi	London-American	1959
White Silver Sands	Bill Black Combo	Hi	London-American	1960
Josephine	Bill Black Combo	Hi	London-American	1960
Ain't That A Shame	Pat Boone	Dot	London	1955
I'll Be Home	Pat Boone	Dot	London	1956
Friendly Persuasion	Pat Boone	Dot	London	1956
Remember You're Mine	Pat Boone	Dot	London	1956
I Almost Lost My Mind	Pat Boone	Dot	London	1956
Love Letters In The Sand	Pat Boone	Dot	London	1957
Don't Forbid Me	Pat Boone	Dot	London	1957
Why, Baby, Why	Pat Boone	Dot	London	1957
April Love	Pat Boone	Dot	London	1958

		US Label	UK Label	Date
A Wonderful Time Up There	Pat Boone	Dot	London	1958
Chérie I Love You	Pat Boone	Dot	London	1958
Moody River	Pat Boone	Dot	London-American	1961
Big Bopper's Wedding/ Chantilly Lace	Big Bopper	Mercury	Pye	1959
I'm Sticking With You	J. Bowen	Roulette	Columbia	1957
You're Sixteen	Johnny Burnette	Liberty	London-American	1960
Way Down Yonder In New Orleans	Freddy Cannon	Swan	Top Rank	1959
I Walk The Line	Johnny Cash	Sun	London	1956
Tequila	Champs	Challenge	London-American	1958
What'd I Say (Parts 1 & 2)	Ray Charles	Atlantic	London-American	1959
Georgia On My Mind	Ray Charles	ABC Paramount	HMV	1960
Hit The Road Jack	Ray Charles	ABC Paramount	HMV	1961
Just A Dream	Jimmy Clanton	Ace	London	1958
A Letter To An Angel	Jimmy Clanton	Ace	London	1958
Ship On A Stormy Sea	Jimmy Clanton	Ace	London-American	1959
Raindrops	Dee Clark	VeeJay	London	1961
Searchin'	Coasters	Atco	London-American	1957
Yakety Yak	Coasters	Atco	London	1958
Charlie Brown	Coasters	Atco	London-American	1959
Poison Ivy	Coasters	Atco	London-American	1959
Along Came Jones	Coasters	Atco	London-American	1959
Sittin' In The Balcony	Eddie Cochran	Liberty	London	1957
Topsy (Part II)	Cozy Cole	Love	London	1958
You Send Me	Sam Cooke	Keen	London	1958
Last Date	Floyd Cramer	RCA Victor	RCA Victor	1960
On The Rebound	Floyd Cramer	RCA Victor	RCA Victor	1961
Sixteen Candles	Crests	Coed	London	1958
That'll Be The Day	Crickets	Brunswick Coral	London	1957
Maybe Baby	Crickets	Brunswick Coral	London	1958
At The Hop	Danny and the Juniors	ABC Paramount	HMV	1958
Splish Splash	Bobby Darin	Atco	London	1958

		US Label	UK Label	Date
Dream Lover	Bobby Darin	Atco	London-American	1959
Queen Of The Hop	Bobby Darin	Atco	London-American	1959
Mack The Knife	Bobby Darin	Atco	London-American	1959
Rockin' Robin	Bobby Day	Class	London	1958
Come Go With Me	Del-Vikings	Dot	London	1957
Little Darlin'	The Diamonds	Mercury	Mercury	1957
A Teenager In Love	Dion and the Belmonts	Laurie	London-American	1959
Runaround Sue	Dion	Laurie	London-American	1961
The Wanderer	Dion	Laurie	London-American	1961
My Heart Is An Open Book	Carl Dobkins Jr	Decca	London-American	1959
Honky Tonk	Bill Doggett	King	Columbia	1956
All By Myself	Fats Domino	Imperial	London	1955
I Can't Go On	Fats Domino	Imperial	London	1955
Ain't That A Shame	Fats Domino	Imperial	London	1955
I'm In Love Again	Fats Domino	Imperial	London	1956
Boll Weevil	Fats Domino	Imperial	London	1956
Blue Monday	Fats Domino	Imperial	London	1956
Blueberry Hill	Fats Domino	Imperial	London	1956
It's You I Love	Fats Domino	Imperial	London	1957
I'm Walkin'	Fats Domino	Imperial	London	1957
I Still Love You	Fats Domino	Imperial	London	1957
Whole Lotta Lovin'	Fats Domino	Imperial	London-American	1960
Walkin' To New Orleans	Fats Domino	Imperial	London-American	1961
Tear Drops Will Fall	Dickie Doo and the Don'ts	Swan	London-American	1959
There Goes My Baby	The Drifters	Atlantic	London-American	1959
Dance With Me/True Love, True Love	The Drifters	Atlantic	London-American	1960
Save The Last Dance For Me	The Drifters	Atlantic	London-American	1960
Rebel Rouser	Duane Eddy	Jamie	London	1958
Ramrod	Duane Eddy	Jamie	London	1958
Cannonball	Duane Eddy	Jamie	London	1958
The Lonely One	Duane Eddy	Jamie	London-American	1959
Peter Gunn	Duane Eddy	Jamie	London-American	1959

		US Label	UK Label	Date
Forty Miles Of Bad Road	Duane Eddy	Jamie	London-American	1959
Shazam	Duane Eddy	Jamie	London-American	1960
Because They're Young	Duane Eddy	Jamie	London-American	1960
Pepe	Duane Eddy	Jamie	London-American	1961
Little Star	The Elegants	Apt	Pye	1958
Bye, Bye Love	Everly Brothers	Cadence	London	1957
Wake Up Little Susie	Everly Brothers	Cadence	London	1957
All I Have To Do Is Dream	Everly Brothers	Cadence	London	1958
Bird Dog/Devoted To You	Everly Brothers	Cadence	London	1958
Problems	Everly Brothers	Cadence	London	1958
Take A Message To Mary	Everly Brothers	Cadence	London-American	1959
(Till) I Kissed You	Everly Brothers	Cadence	London-American	1959
Cathy's Clown	Everly Brothers	Warner Brothers	London-American	1960
Walk Right Back/Ebony Eyes	Everly Brothers	Warner Brothers	London-American	1961
Come Softly To Me	The Fleetwoods	Dolton	London-American	1959
Mr Blue	The Fleetwoods	Dolton	London-American	1959
Sea Cruise	Frankie Ford	Ace	London-American	1959
Who's Sorry Now	Connie Francis	MGM	MGM	1958
My Happiness	Connie Francis	MGM	MGM	1959
Lipstick On Your Collar	Connie Francis	MGM	MGM	1959
Among My Souvenirs	Connie Francis	MGM	MGM	1959
Mama/Teddy	Connie Francis	MGM	MGM	1960
Everybody's Somebody's Fool	Connie Francis	MGM	MGM	1960
Together	Connie Francis	MGM	MGM	1961
Many Tears Ago	Connie Francis	MGM	MGM	1961
Where The Boys Are	Connie Francis	MGM	MGM	1961
Butterfly	Charlie Gracie	Cameo	Parlophone	1957
Rock Around The Clock	Bill Haley	Decca	Brunswick	1955
Shake Rattle And Roll	Bill Haley	Decca	Brunswick	1955
Kansas City	Wilbert Harrison	Fury	Top Rank	1959
Peggy Sue	Buddy Holly	Coral	Coral	1958
It Doesn't Matter Anymore	Buddy Holly	Coral	Coral	1959
Alley-Oop	The Hollywood Argyles	Lute	London-American	1960

		US Label	UK Label	Date
Sorry (I Ran All The Way Home)	Impalas	Cub	MGM	1958
Fever	Little Willie John	King	Columbia	1956
Talk To Me, Talk To Me	Little Willie John	King	Columbia	1958
Red River Rock	Johnny and the Hurricanes	Warwick	London-American	1959
(You've Got To) Move Two Mountains	Marv Johnson	UA	London-American	1960
Handy Man	Jimmy Jones	Cub	MGM	1960
Good Timin'	Jimmy Jones	Cub	MGM	1960
Raunchy	Bill Justis	Phillips International	London	1958
When	Kalin Twins	Decca	Brunswick	1958
Party Doll	Buddy Knox	Roulette	Columbia	1957
Hula Love	Buddy Knox	Roulette	Columbia	1957
Rock Your Little Baby To Sleep	Buddy Knox	Roulette	Columbia	1957
Sweet Nothin's	Brenda Lee	Decca	Brunswick	1960
I'm Sorry/That's All You Gotta Do	Brenda Lee	Decca	Brunswick	1960
Tossin' And Turnin'	Bobby Lewis	Beltone	London-American	1961
Whole Lotta Shakin' Goin' On	Jerry Lee Lewis	Sun	London	1957
Great Balls Of Fire	Jerry Lee Lewis	Sun	London	1958
Breathless	Jerry Lee Lewis	Sun	London	1958
High School Confidential	Jerry Lee Lewis	Sun	London	1958
Green Door	Jim Lowe	Dot	London	1957
Susie Darlin'	Robin Luke	Dot	London	1958
Why Do Fools Fall In Love	Frankie Lymon and the Teenagers	Gee	Columbia	1956
A Lover's Question	Clyde McPhatter	Atlantic	London	1958
Teenagers' Romance	Ricky Nelson	Verve	HMV	1957
Stood Up	Ricky Nelson	Imperial	London	1957
Waitin' In School	Ricky Nelson	Imperial	London	1957
Be Bop Baby	Ricky Nelson	Imperial	London	1958
Poor Little Fool	Ricky Nelson	Imperial	London	1958
Lonesome Town	Ricky Nelson	Imperial	London	1958
Believe What You Say	Ricky Nelson	Imperial	London	1958
It's Late/Never Be Anyone Else But You	Ricky Nelson	Imperial	London-American	1959
Travellin' Man/Hello Mary Lou	Ricky Nelson	Imperial	London-American	1960
Only The Lonely	Roy Orbison	Monument	London-American	1960
Runnin' Scared	Roy Orbison	Monument	London-American	1961

		US Label	UK Label	Date
Cryin'	Roy Orbison	Monument	London-American	1961
Earth Angel	The Penguins	Dooto	London	1957
Blue Suede Shoes	Carl Perkins	Sun	London	1956
Sea of Love	Phil Phillips	Mercury	Mercury	1959
Only You	The Platters	Mercury	Pye	1955
The Great Pretender	The Platters	Mercury	Pye	1955
My Prayer	The Platters	Mercury	Pye	1956
Twilight Time	The Platters	Mercury	Pye	1958
Smoke Gets In Your Eyes	The Platters	Mercury	Pye	1959
Heartbreak Hotel	Elvis Presley	RCA	RCA	1956
I Want You, I Need You, I Love You	Elvis Presley	RCA	RCA	1956
Love Me Tender	Elvis Presley	RCA	RCA	1956
All Shook Up	Elvis Presley	RCA	RCA	1957
Don't Be Cruel/Hound Dog	Elvis Presley	RCA	RCA	1957
Too Much	Elvis Presley	RCA	RCA	1957
Teddy Bear/Loving You	Elvis Presley	RCA	RCA	1957
Jailhouse Rock	Elvis Presley	RCA	RCA	1957
Wear My Ring Around Your Neck	Elvis Presley	RCA	RCA	1958
Don't	Elvis Presley	RCA	RCA	1958
I Got Stung	Elvis Presley	RCA	RCA	1958
Hard Headed Woman	Elvis Presley	RCA	RCA	1958
A Fool Such As I	Elvis Presley	RCA	RCA	1958
Stuck On You	Elvis Presley	RCA	RCA	1959
It's Now or Never	Elvis Presley	RCA	RCA	1960
Are You Lonesome Tonight	Elvis Presley	RCA	RCA	1960
Surrender	Elvis Presley	RCA	RCA	1961
Can't Help Falling In Love	Elvis Presley	RCA	RCA	1961
Running Bear	Johnny Preston	Mercury	Mercury	1960
Stagger Lee	Lloyd Price	ABC Paramount	HMV	1959
Silhouettes	The Rays	Cameo	London	1957
Livin' Doll	Cliff Richard		Columbia	1959
Tutti Frutti	Little Richard	Specialty	London	1955
Long Tall Sally	Little Richard	Specialty	London	1956
Rip It Up	Little Richard	Specialty	London	1956
Lucille	Little Richard	Specialty	London	1957
Jenny, Jenny	Little Richard	Specialty	London	1957
Keep A Knockin'	Little Richard	Specialty	London	1957
Good Golly Miss Molly	Little Richard	Specialty	London	1958
Teenage Crush	Tommy Sands	Capitol	Capitol	1957
My True Love/Leroy	Jack Scott	Carlton	London	1958
What In The World's Come Over You	Jack Scott	Top Rank	Top Rank	1960

		US Label	UK Label	Date
I Go Ape	Neil Sedaka	RCA	RCA	1959
Oh Carol	Neil Sedaka	RCA	RCA	1959
Apache	The Shadows		Columbia	1960
Get A Job	The Silhouettes	Ember	London	1958
Rockin' Pneumonia And The Boogie Woogie Flu	Huey Smith and the Clowns	Ace	London	1957
Wheels	String-A-Longs	Warwick	London-American	1961
To Know Him Is To Love Him	Teddy Bears	Dore	London	1958
It's Only Make-Believe	Conway Twitty	MGM	MGM	1958
Lonely Boy Blue	Conway Twitty	MGM	MGM	1960
Donna/La Bamba	Ritchie Valens	Del-Fi	London	1958
Walk, Don't Run	The Ventures	Dolton	London-American	1960
Perfidia	The Ventures	Dolton	London-American	1961
Be-Bop-A-Lula	Gene Vincent	Capitol	Capitol	1956
Blue-jean Bop	Gene Vincent	Capitol	Capitol	1956
Wear My Ring	Gene Vincent	Capitol	Capitol	1957
Tragedy	Thomas Wayne	Fernwood	London-American	1961
Short Fat Fanny	Larry Williams	Specialty	London	1957
Bony Maronie	Larry Williams	Specialty	London	1957
Hearts Of Stone	Otis Williams and the Charms	DeLuxe	London	1955
Ivory Tower	Otis Williams and the Charms	DeLuxe	London	1956
Lonely Teardrops	Jackie Wilson	Brunswick	Coral	1959
Night/Doggin' Around	Jackie Wilson	Brunswick	Coral	1960